"This outstanding, state-of-the-art treatment program is an essential resource for all clinicians helping all adolescents reclaim and rebuild their lives after the devastating effects of trauma and addiction."

—**Kim T. Mueser, PhD**, director of the Center for Psychiatric Rehabilitation and professor of occupational therapy, psychology, and psychiatry at Boston University

"The world is witnessing an explosion of mindfulness possibilities, but mindfulness is not a generic, one-size-fits-all fix. The process and delivery of a mindfulness-based program demands subtle adjustments in dosage and approach, including knowledge about how mindfulness practice may impact specific populations. Fortuna and Vallejo bring mature experience and deep wisdom to the task. By blending mindfulness with therapeutic interventions, such as cognitive restructuring and motivational interviewing (among others), this guide is a trustworthy companion in meeting your adolescent clients in skillful, responsive, and life-affirming ways."

—**Lynn Koerbel, MPH**, associate director of the Oasis Institute for Mindfulness-Based Professional Education and Training at the Center for Mindfulness in Medicine, Health Care, and Society at the University of Massachusetts Medical School, coauthor of *A Mindfulness-Based Stress Reduction Workbook for Anxiety*, and teacher of MBSR since 2005

"Adolescents with complex trauma lack a basic sense of safety in the world and an understanding of others as responsive and trustworthy. It is through relationship that we develop the capacity to be seen and to be known. This wonderful guide helps teens restore safety and predictability within their bodies, a sense of agency in the world, and an understanding of themselves as worthy of care."

—**David Schouela**, staff yoga teacher at the Trauma Center at Justice Resource Institute (JRI), Brookline, MA

"As a father, it is very comforting to know that two very dedicated, wise, and loving clinicians have written a hands-on treatment manual for adolescents living with PTSD and addiction. The practices of mindfulness have the power to transform and heal the wounded heart. Thank you, Lisa and Zayda, for loving and caring for our children."

—**Bob Stahl, PhD**, coauthor of *A Mindfulness-Based Stress Reduction Workbook, Living with Your Heart Wide Open, Calming the Rush of Panic, A Mindfulness-Based Stress Reduction Workbook for Anxiety*, and *MBSR Every Day*

"This book is just what I was looking for to assist me in my work with adolescents struggling with PTSD and substance abuse. What I really appreciated was that the authors offer clear and useful solutions for working with teens that may never have practiced any type of self-soothing techniques. Not only does the book provide concrete explanations of strategies such as mindfulness and meditations, but it also gives step-by-step guidelines as to how to implement them into my practice. As a social worker in an urban middle school, this book has given me intervention techniques that will assist the students so that they can calm down to the point that they are able to identify the underlying feelings that are causing them to act out in school."

—**Stacy L. Homan, LICSW**, School Adjustment Counselor, Worcester East Middle School, Worcester, MA

Treating Co-occurring Adolescent PTSD and Addiction

Mindfulness-Based Cognitive Therapy for Adolescents with Trauma and Substance-Abuse Disorders

Lisa R. Fortuna, MD | Zayda Vallejo, MLitt

CONTEXT PRESS
An Imprint of New Harbinger Publications, Inc.

Publisher's Note

This publication is designed to provide accurate and authoritative information in regard to the subject matter covered. It is sold with the understanding that the publisher is not engaged in rendering psychological, financial, legal, or other professional services. If expert assistance or counseling is needed, the services of a competent professional should be sought.

Distributed in Canada by Raincoast Books

Context Press
An Imprint of New Harbinger Publications, Inc.
5674 Shattuck Avenue
Oakland, CA 94609
www.newharbinger.com

FSC www.fsc.org MIX Paper from responsible sources FSC® C011935

RAINFOREST ALLIANCE CERTIFIED

Cover design by Amy Shoup; Acquired by Jess O'Brien;
Edited by Rona Bernstein; Indexed by James Minkin

Library of Congress Cataloging-in-Publication Data

Fortuna, Lisa R.
Treating co-occurring adolescent PTSD and addiction : mindfulness-based cognitive therapy for adolescents with trauma and substance-abuse disorders / Lisa R. Fortuna, MD, MPH, MDiv, and Zayda Vallejo, MLitt ; foreword by Florence Meleo-Meyer, MS, MA.
pages cm
Includes bibliographical references and index.
ISBN 978-1-62625-133-5 (paperback) -- ISBN 978-1-62625-134-2 (pdf e-book) -- ISBN 978-1-62625-135-9 (epub) 1. Post-traumatic stress disorder in adolescence--Treatment. 2. Substance abuse--Treatment. 3. Cognitive therapy for teenagers. I. Vallejo, Zayda. II. Title.
RJ506.P55F67 2015
616.85'2100835--dc23

2015018136

Printed in the United States of America

17 16 15

10 9 8 7 6 5 4 3 2 1 First printing

To H. E. Choegyal Rinpoche, VIII, who embodies unconditional love —Zayda

To my grandmother "Bolito" —Lisa

Contents

Foreword

The guiding intention and focus of this book is essentially compassion in action. The authors, Lisa Fortuna, MD, and Zayda Vallejo, MLitt (Oxon), have defined a potential pathway for adolescents to achieve greater health through mindfulness-based cognitive therapy for adolescents with trauma and substance-abuse disorders (MBCT-Dual). The book offers the therapist and caregiver a host of tools to deliver a program that has the potential to skillfully alleviate the suffering of adolescents who have been hurt multiple times in their lives. Numbing is one way an adolescent may attempt to cope with the anguish of intrusive thoughts and emotions following the shock of trespassing encounters of physical, emotional, and sexual abuse. Commonly, drugs and alcohol are the means teens employ to find relief, and in turn become another source of suffering as addiction. These methods, of course, make teens more susceptible to deeper trauma, expose them to dangerous situations, and complicate a lifelong trap of avoidance. The information and skillful guidance in this book offer a pathway to greater ease and health that focuses on recovery from trauma and addiction while also establishing the groundwork for greater self-esteem and constructive life skills.

Through psychoeducation, mindfulness practices, and cognitive strategies, the adolescent is offered a program that is much more than a technique. Through the strong and ongoing practice of mindfulness, the adolescent is introduced to a way of living. Mindfulness is not just a practice of meditation but an intrinsic human awareness in all human beings. Through mindfulness meditation, one discovers presence—a presence which can never be diminished, no matter how terribly one has been hurt. The practice engages the adolescent in the discovery of this essential human capacity that is most often overlooked—innate wholeness. Mindfulness honors and strengthens what is most deep, wise, and kind within one's own being. The practice of mindfulness allows this innate capacity to be known. Through this, the adolescent has the potential to directly experience the statement by Jon Kabat-Zinn, PhD, founder of the Mindfulness-Based Stress Reduction (MBSR) program at the University of Massachusetts over 35 years ago: "there is more right with you than there is wrong, no matter how ill or how hopeless you may feel" (Kabat-Zinn, 2013, p. 2).

As the adolescent recognizes and practices the potential ability to know a sensation as a sensation, a thought as a thought, and an emotion as an emotion, he or she is awake to the content of these life experiences and their constant movement and pulls. This knowing can strengthen the teen to be more familiar and intimate with the conditioning of one's inner and outer life as well as offer methods to "hold steady" when the urge to escape pain becomes intensely compelling. The practice of mindfulness allows for this recognition and offers skills and tools to meet and work with challenging self-opinions and the pull of less effective methods of coping.

The very nature of this practice engenders a sense of greater safety and empowerment as teens are guided step by step to develop self-knowledge and the means to work with trauma symptoms as they emerge. Meeting one's life this way can build greater stability, self-compassion, and forgiveness. From working with one's own hurt, painful memories, and patterns of avoidance and reactivity, the adolescent can cultivate greater steadiness and compassion in his or her responses to others.

As a therapy tool, this manual has great potential to inform and enable the health care provider with methodology and practices to honor the whole person of the adolescent.

Information on traumatic stress, neuroscience, addiction, cognitive restructuring, steps of recovery, and mindfulness presented in clear, age-appropriate language offers the clinician both background in the program and ways to introduce it to teens. The mindfulness practices are clearly written and will offer natural support for the clinician as she or he introduces these to adolescents. It is always important, though, that the clinician practice mindfulness personally in order to share the practice with another. In this sense again, mindfulness is not a technique but a way of living. When it is lived, it can be shared from natural experience and not just as ideas in a book.

The authors, Dr. Lisa Fortuna and Zayda Vallejo, bring to the creation of this book personal and professional lives dedicated to the relief of suffering.

Lisa Fortuna, MD, MPH, is a board certified child and adolescent psychiatrist and diplomate of the American Board of Addiction Medicine. Her research interests include Latino and immigrant mental health services, post-traumatic stress disorder, and adolescent substance abuse and co-occurring disorders. She is currently working on therapy development for Latino immigrants as well as adapting evidence-based interventions for community and school-based prevention and mental health services for youth, including those at risk of gang or juvenile detention involvement.

Zayda Vallejo, MLitt (Oxon), is a certified MBSR teacher who trained and taught at the Center for Mindfulness in Medicine, Health Care, and Society at the University of Massachusetts Medical School. Her dedication, skill, and warmth are acknowledged by the many students in her MBSR classes as well as by the educators and clinicians who engaged in her Mindfulness-Based Professional Education and Training courses through the Oasis Institute. Her broad teaching experience includes working with mothers new to recovery, adolescents, and the general public. She has taught programs and has authored a book on relapse prevention, and she has also been involved in several research projects. As director of HeartWell Institute, she continues to introduce practices which cultivate awareness and compassion in alignment with her deep intention to relieve suffering and uplift the lives of many.

This book is an important contribution to improving and more directly addressing the needs of adolescents who are at risk. From the practice and deep caring of both authors, this book gives guidance to see and meet those who so often feel invisible and without hope. May many be served and find the wholeness that they truly are.

—Florence Meleo-Meyer, MS, MA
Director, Oasis Institute for Mindfulness-Based Professional Education and Training
Center for Mindfulness in Medicine, Health Care, and Society
University of Massachusetts Medical School

Acknowledgments

The development of this manual was supported in part by a Mentored Patient-Oriented Research Career Development Award from the National Institute on Drug Abuse (K23 DA14009-01) to Dr. Lisa Fortuna.

Immense thanks to Rona Bernstein, our copyeditor, for her impeccable attention to detail, and to Jess O'Brien, Vicraj Gill, and New Harbinger Publications for their support and commitment in working with us to bring this work to its fruition. Thanks also to Michelle Porche, who engineered the audio for the book, and Rachel Arrey, who read the recorded meditations.

Lisa's acknowledgments: Special thanks to Donna Massey, Katherine Perkins, Arden Bowser, and Community HealthLink in Worcester, MA, for all of their assistance in the research and development of this manual and for their commitment to the well-being of young people. Special thanks to Drs. Margarita Alegria, Kim Mueser, Stanley Rosenberg, and Douglas Ziedonis for their mentorship and guidance with cognitive behavioral therapy for post-traumatic stress disorder (CBT for PTSD). I want to offer my most profound thank you to Dr. Michelle Porche for her hard work assisting with the research on the therapy model reflected in this manual and her never-ending support and patience. Finally, I want to offer a special thank you to all of the adolescents whose boldness and honesty have taught me so much and have inspired this book.

Zayda's acknowledgments: I am enormously grateful to Jon Kabat-Zinn for creating a blueprint for transformation, balance, and self-compassion. Jon's brilliance, insight, and love for his work have informed and inspired me in my teaching and in my life. Saki Santorelli has been an extraordinary teacher and friend and has provided brilliant and pointed guidance all along the way. Florence Meleo-Meyer (whom I like to call "Mother Earth") has guided and supported me with immense patience and dedication. Melissa Blacker has been a mentor for many years and was the teacher with whom I cotaught my first Mindfulness-Based Stress Reduction (MBSR) program in 2003 to a group of women in early recovery from substance abuse. Elana Rosenbaum, my neighbor and dear heart sister, has also been a guiding light. I am most grateful to my other colleagues at the University of Massachusetts

Center for Mindfulness—Lynn Koerbel, Pam Erdamn, Bob Stahl, Rob Smith, Carolyn West, Paul Galvin, Jim Kolosi, Colleen Camenisch, and Diana Kamila. Additionally, Liz Hoge, Britta Holtzel, Hannah Reese, Sara Lazar, and Zev Schuman-Olivier from the Harvard University Medical School have all provided opportunities for me to contribute to the mindfulness research community. I thank my colleagues on the faculty of the Transforming Trauma Initiative at the Garrison Institute, with special thanks to Sharon Salzberg and Diana Rose, and I extend deep thanks to the many other colleagues who have traveled with me on the path of mindfulness. I owe a tremendous debt to my dear husband, Bob Lenhardt, who has patiently supported my growth in this field and edited papers until late at night, and to my son Mark A. Rojas for his openhearted support and boundless love.

Introduction

Welcome to this valuable and practical opportunity to engage adolescents in a mindfulness-based approach to recovery from trauma and addictions.

Mindfulness-based cognitive therapy for adolescents with trauma and substance-abuse disorders (MBCT-Dual) is an integrated approach that combines mindfulness practices and cognitive therapy to treat adolescents with post-traumatic stress disorder (PTSD) and addictions. Practitioners working with adolescents with co-occurring disorders in outpatient, residential, and other clinical practice settings must provide quality therapy and psychosocial interventions. Efficacious interventions are also necessary in juvenile detention centers and other programs providing services to vulnerable adolescents living in high-risk environments and dealing with unsafe circumstances. The impetus for the research and development behind this therapy model and manual was the desire to meet this need and help guide clinicians in providing a therapeutic and resiliency-building intervention for adolescents with these co-occurring disorders, also referred to as dual diagnosis.

MBCT-Dual presents a wide array of resources and tools that can be modified and adapted to reduce trauma symptoms and build a sense of safety for clients. As part of the MBCT-Dual intervention, adolescents gain practice in mindfulness, which provides them with greater attention to and awareness of their current sensations, thoughts, feelings, and surroundings. Practicing mindfulness helps adolescents begin to recognize their habitual patterns of thinking and acting and to respond to these thoughts and actions in more nonjudgmental, kind, and helpful ways, fostering general well-being and enhanced overall functioning. Ultimately, the adolescent is able to display self-compassion and compassion toward others.

As you use this manual you will apply the following three strategies, which overlap and build upon one another:

1. **Psychoeducation:** Providing age-appropriate information about the brain, traumatic stress, and addiction symptoms, utilizing interactive approaches and supporting motivation for treatment.

2. **Practicing mindfulness and building awareness:** Providing an opportunity for guided practice in mindfulness through exercises such as awareness

of sounds, body scanning interspersed with movement, awareness of breath meditation, eating meditation, mindful walking, and mindfulness in daily activities.

3. **Teaching cognitive strategies:** Providing guidance in learning and applying cognitive skills, such as cognitive restructuring, to facilitate recovery from addiction and foster constructive, compassionate responding to trauma-related sensations, thoughts, feelings, and actions.

The manual is divided into chapters that will assist you, the clinician, in understanding the theory and practice behind each component of MBCT-Dual and in conducting therapy sessions. Each therapy session guide includes an outline highlighting the main goals and a guiding script for conducting that meeting. It is recommended that you preview these before each session and that you follow the manual more closely while you are learning the model. As you become more comfortable, you are encouraged to use your own language and adapt these methods in creative ways to cover the material. Still, it is important to successfully build the adolescent's mindfulness practice and use of cognitive strategies during the course of therapy. As will be further emphasized, it is highly recommended that as a clinician you maintain your own regular mindfulness practice in order to draw upon your personal experience and embody the attitudes and behaviors that you are inviting the adolescents to cultivate.

This manual contains the following sections:

Overview of the program: Chapter 1 provides an orientation to the program components and its treatment goals as well as information about working with adolescents using this approach. Chapter 2 addresses the specifics of intervention, including pacing treatment, incorporating role-plays, and addressing trauma and addictions in an integrated fashion, illustrating these concepts through case studies. In chapter 3, techniques are presented for motivating and engaging adolescents and supporting their readiness for change. Chapter 4 addresses the use of MBCT-Dual with other common co-occurring disorders including attention deficit/hyperactivity disorder (ADHD) and depression, and chapter 5 addresses the use of mindfulness for improving communication.

Therapy guide: Chapter 6 provides general considerations and guidelines for structuring MBCT-Dual meetings, followed by chapter 7, which offers detailed therapy session guidance. This final chapter includes the main objectives for each session along with scripts and references to the handouts in the *Client Workbook* that will guide you in using the practice exercises and activities in each session.

Appendices: Appendices A, B, C, and D include scripts for guiding mindfulness meditations, selected MBCT-Dual tools, guidelines for incorporating role-play into therapy sessions, and suggestions for using poetry in mindfulness practices.

Client Workbook: Exercise handouts in the accompanying workbook correspond to the therapy sessions described in chapter 7 and cover the essential skills adolescents will learn during the therapy sessions.

Guided meditations and downloadable copies of the *Client Workbook* are available online at http://www.newharbinger.com/31335. Please see the very back of this book for more details.

Part 1

Understanding Mindfulness-Based Cognitive Therapy for Adolescents with Trauma and Substance-Abuse Disorders

Chapter 1

An Integrated Approach to the Treatment of Trauma and Addictions in Adolescents

With mindfulness, you can establish yourself in the present in order to touch the wonders of life that are available in that moment.

—Thich Nhat Hanh

Mindfulness-based cognitive therapy for adolescents with trauma and substance-abuse disorders (MBCT-Dual) was partly developed through a research program funded by the National Institute on Drug Abuse to better understand how to address the treatment needs of adolescents with co-occurring post-traumatic and substance abuse problems using cognitive therapy. It is designed to meet the needs of adolescents with symptoms of post-traumatic stress disorder (PTSD) related to a variety of traumatic life events including exposure to community or domestic violence, physical or sexual abuse, and chronic stressors. Feedback from adolescents and their parents, as well as previous research with adults and adolescents, has been instrumental in developing this cognitive therapy (CT) approach and integrating it with mindfulness (Amaro & Vallejo, 2008; Fortuna, Porche, & Ziedonis, 2013; Kilpatrick et al., 2000; Lipschitz et al., 2003; McGovern et al., 2009; Rosenberg, Jankowski, Fortuna, Rosenberg, & Mueser, 2011; Stevens, Murphy, & McKnight, 2003; Vallejo & Amaro, 2009).

This therapy takes a resiliency-building approach. Resiliency is a dynamic process whereby an individual is able to employ and exhibit positive behavioral adaptations in the face of adversity (Luthar, Cicchetti, & Becker, 2000). Many young people have contributed their time as participants in our therapy study and have offered feedback regarding how it has helped them respond to adversity. Most have endured multiple traumatic experiences in their lives. All have had to develop their own coping skills for living in a chronically stressful and high-risk environment. The therapy approach presented in this manual is most effective as part of a comprehensive intervention for adolescents that addresses their multiple emotional, relational, psychosocial, and educational needs.

Who Is This Treatment For?

This therapy was designed and studied for the treatment of co-occurring PTSD and substance-abuse disorders in adolescents over thirteen years of age. The substances used by adolescents in our studies include alcohol, stimulants (e.g., cocaine, methylphenidate), opiates (e.g., heroin), over-the-counter and prescription drugs (e.g., Oxycontin, Percocet, benzodiazepines, cough medicine), and new synthetic drugs such as Spice or K2 (Fortuna et al., 2013). In identifying adolescents appropriate for this therapy, we have defined substance abuse as drug or alcohol use which interferes with an individual's functioning and/or results in social, academic, and/or legal difficulty. The treatment has been tested with boys and girls, and versions have been developed in both English and Spanish. The program can be useful for adolescents who have, in addition to PTSD and substance abuse, other commonly associated challenges such as depression, anxiety, ADHD, or disruptive behavior disorders. A history of multiple stressors and trauma experiences was common among participants in our therapy studies.

Why Did We Undertake an Integrated Dual-Diagnosis Approach?

Substance abuse is a common problem experienced by youth with PTSD. Combined, these disorders have been found to potentially worsen the course of each individual disorder (Kilpatrick et al., 2000; Lipschitz et al., 2003). Substance abuse is a risk factor for traumatic experiences, and conversely, PTSD symptoms can exacerbate the use of substances. A self-medication model explains how youth with preexisting trauma and PTSD may develop substance-use disorders (SUDs) including abuse and misuse of both illicit and prescription drugs. For adolescents who have symptoms of PTSD, intrusive trauma-related thoughts can elicit intense psychological distress (e.g., terror, anger, sadness, shame) as well as physiological hyperarousal (e.g., increased heart rate, startle response, sleep disturbance). Drugs and alcohol may offer a readily available method for avoiding distressing emotions and negative physical arousal. Addiction may result from the need for long-lasting avoidance of psychological distress as well as prevention of negative mood states associated with drug withdrawal.

It is also important to consider how SUDs may reinforce preexisting PTSD symptoms. Some research indicates that youth with SUDs are at increased risk of experiencing interpersonal violence, which could serve as a reminder of previous abuse or trauma and contribute to worsening PTSD symptoms (Kilpatrick et al., 2000; Lipschitz et al., 2003; Stevens et al., 2003). For example, youth who resort to exchanging sexual acts in order to obtain drugs are at heightened risk of sexual and physical coercion or assault, which contributes to further traumatization and can serve to maintain or exacerbate PTSD symptoms. Thus, for some youth, abuse-related PTSD and SUDs create a vicious cycle with increasingly negative consequences.

Who Can Use This Manual?

This manualized treatment is designed to be delivered by a trained mental health or substance abuse clinician, ideally one who has experience in clinical practice with adolescents. It is an appropriate treatment model for outpatient school-based health centers, substance abuse programs, and other community health and mental health settings. The research we conducted for the development of this treatment manual was carried out in these types of settings. Clinicians who focus on either mental health problems or addictions can implement this treatment to help their adolescent clients. We highly recommend two strategies: (1) practice closely with the manual, especially when first starting to use the therapy model; and (2) begin and sustain your own mindfulness practice—this is essential for developing mindfulness practice with adolescents.

What's Different About This Approach?

The manual differs from some other CT models for treating PTSD in that it integrates mindfulness tools and practices and does not include therapeutic exposure (i.e., exposure of the client to the feared object or context without any danger), which is often applied in the treatment of PTSD and anxiety disorders. The rationale for employing the CT technique of cognitive restructuring (CR), or reframing, as the primary ingredient—and not exposure—is based on several considerations: (1) a randomized clinical study of this therapy approach used with adults with severe mental illness suggested a clinical benefit of using primarily CR (Mueser et al., 2008); (2) providers who treat adolescents have highlighted concerns about employing exposure techniques with this population, including the possible triggering of drug or alcohol use. Controlled research comparing CR and exposure treatments for PTSD in adults has indicated that the approaches can be equally effective and superior to simple relaxation techniques (Marks et al., 1998). And while research regarding the comparative efficacy of exposure and CR for PTSD in adolescents has not yet been conducted, in our current treatment study we have seen reductions in PTSD symptoms to nonclinical levels, comparable to those reported in exposure-based approaches.

In addition, we have integrated mindfulness concepts and practices as a basis of, and complement to, the CT. We did this because we and others have found that many adolescents, especially those with dual diagnosis (having trauma-related symptoms and an addiction disorder), often find it challenging to slow down their automatic reactions, to exercise "choice" in their life, and to be aware of their own thoughts and feelings so that they can respond appropriately instead of reacting reflexively or automatically (Segal, Williams, & Teasdale, 2002). Mindfulness assists individuals in developing awareness (Kabat-Zinn, 1990/2013) and attention (Siegel, 2010). These, in turn, are helpful in CT, but more importantly offer the adolescent an opportunity to make different choices—for example to utilize new behaviors for managing cravings and impulses or responding to trauma triggers (Segal, Williams, & Teasdale, 2002).

What Is Mindfulness?

Mindfulness is integrated and discussed throughout this therapy, so it is important to more clearly define what we mean by it. The most widely used definition of mindfulness is by Jon Kabat-Zinn, who describes it as "the awareness that arises by paying attention on purpose, in the present moment, and non-judgmentally" (Kabat-Zinn, 2013, p. 4). In other words, "Mindfulness meditation is a consciousness discipline revolving around a particular way of paying attention in one's life. It can be most simply described as the intentional cultivation of nonjudgmental moment-to-moment awareness" (Kabat-Zinn, 1996, p. 161).

Mindfulness is a faculty that we all possess but hardly ever exercise. It is the capacity to pay conscious attention, with the intention to sustain focus on whatever we are doing, with a sense of exploration and acceptance. Acceptance does not mean resignation. Acceptance is the ability to see as clearly as possible what is happening, without trying to change it in any way or make it go away, and without frills, embellishment, or the constant narrative that seems to accompany all that we see or do.

Mindfulness is similar to the process of looking at ourselves in the mirror. The mirror reflects our face exactly as it is at that moment. It does not reflect how our face looked yesterday or five minutes earlier, or how it will look tomorrow or the day after. Mindfulness is a dynamic process of looking at things as they are. It is also relational. It can be described as the capacity to relate to or work with what is happening with spaciousness, kindness, and softness. Although we cannot always change the world we inhabit or those around us, we can change the way we perceive, appraise, and work with situations.

Mindfulness is the capacity to live our life to the fullest, to be present in our life exactly as it is and not how we want it to be. The awareness that is developed with mindfulness is not a harsh, cold awareness. It is the state or presence of knowing what is happening and observing what unfolds with a sense of exploration and curiosity, with kindness and compassion for ourselves and those around us (Salzberg, 2013). The intention is to befriend and become familiar with whatever happens to arise cognitively or physically.

Mindfulness practices help us cultivate the ability to pause and bring awareness to the present moment experience. From that clarity comes the ability to choose how to behave instead of succumbing to reactive patterns of thoughts and behaviors. Mindfulness develops our ability to reframe an experience and see it in a wider context, and also to develop the "muscle" of attention. It helps us to manage psychological or physical discomfort using the breath or any other object of awareness as a point of focus.

Mindfulness increases our awareness of how our body experiences emotions and the triggers that activate them (Bechara & Naqvi, 2004). Becoming aware of our emotions is the first step in regulating them. Mindfulness of body sensations can provide important information about the signature of emotional states and can allow individuals with PTSD to closely observe signs of both physical and cognitive hyperarousal (e.g., tension in the body, narratives associated with anger, tolerance to pain, startle response, and agitation). It can also help bring curiosity and awareness to self-destructive impulses without the urge to act on them. In neuropsychological terms, it helps to activate the parasympathetic nervous system, which acts as a brake.

Mindfulness also works with the hypoarousal symptoms of avoidance by allowing individuals to move gently toward the difficulty, stop when it gets overwhelming, and not "force" anything to happen. Mark Williams and Danny Penman (2011) connected avoidance with the "doing mode" and approaching with the "being mode":

> Being mode encourages you to "approach" the very things that you feel like avoiding; it invites you to take a friendly interest in your most difficult states of mind. Mindfulness does not say "don't worry" or "don't be sad."

> Instead it acknowledges your fear and your sadness, your fatigue and exhaustion, and encourages you to "turn toward" these feelings and whatever emotions are threatening to engulf you. This compassionate approach gradually dissipates the power of your negative feelings. (p. 41–42)

The following is a case example of the use of mindfulness to help change deeply ingrained habits:

Lilia

Lilia, a seventeen-year-old mother of three living in a residential treatment center, mentioned that her best friend had died from a drug overdose the weekend before. Her first reaction was to do what she had always done when faced with a crisis. She went to her room, lay down, and covered her body and head with a blanket. In the past, she would remain in bed for two or three days at a time. She would not eat, change her clothes, bathe, or answer the door or the telephone. Family and friends would take over her obligations as best they could, and many times they would take her children to their homes to care for them.

This time, however, after being in bed for a short while, Lilia said she remembered the voice of the mindfulness instructor in her head saying, *You cannot stop your thoughts, but you do not have to act on them, and if you do not hold on to a thought, it will move like a cloud, another thought will arise, and you can continue doing this with all the thoughts that arise in your mind.* Lilia became aware of the thought that was present and said *next* to that thought and those that followed. She got up and began doing whatever she needed to do. Several times that weekend she found herself in bed, ready to disappear from the world, and every time she said to herself, *I don't have to listen to this thought that I must stay in bed or the thought that life is meaningless*, and to each thought she kept saying to herself, *next, next, next.* She encouraged herself, got up, and resumed her activities. Lilia said, "This was the first time in my entire life that I could continue to live my life, feeling the pain but without isolating."

Cognitive Therapy

CT has been shown to be very helpful in the treatment of adolescent depression and anxiety disorders (Cohen, Mannarino, & Staron, 2006; Cohen, Mannarino, Zhitova, & Capone, 2003; Dorsey, Briggs, & Woods, 2011; Hamblen et al., 2009;

James, Soler, & Weatherall, 2005). CR, which involves teaching people how to identify and modify the thought or belief underlying a feeling such as sadness or worry, is a widely used CT approach for helping people deal with upsetting feelings, including those related to traumatic experiences. An underlying premise of CT is that certain patterns of automatic thinking can have a direct impact on how we feel. A common example is as follows: When a friend does not wave back after we wave hello, our emotional reaction depends on whether we think he is not doing so because (a) he did not see us, or (b) he purposefully ignored us. The former thought leads to little sadness, whereas the latter triggers automatic thoughts of his wrongdoing and provokes considerable sadness or anger. Automatic thoughts are triggered by our perceptions and experiences. These thoughts work so automatically, in fact, that at times we do not even notice their content yet are left with the sadness or anger. The CR approach is complemented by the mindfulness approach and its emphasis on perception as key to a balanced life. This is presented as mindful problem-focused and emotion-focused coping and is based on the perspective that how we see or "do not see" things will affect how we think and behave.

CT can also be very helpful with recovery from addictions (Carroll et al., 2009; Hides, Samet, & Lubman, 2010; Kabat-Zinn, 2005; Kaminer, Burleson, & Goldberger, 2002) by assisting individuals in identifying factors that lead to substance use and replacing negative behaviors with positive habits. For example, for each instance of cannabis use, the adolescent can practice identifying the thoughts, feelings, bodily sensations, and circumstances that occur around, before, and after the cannabis use. Early in treatment, this plays a critical role in assessing the determinants, or high-risk situations, that are likely to lead to drug use and provides insights into some of the reasons the adolescent may be using drugs (e.g., to cope with interpersonal difficulties, to experience risk or euphoria not otherwise attainable, or to celebrate). Later in treatment, CT approaches may help the individual identify those situations or states that remain difficult to cope with and determine an effective response or behavioral strategy.

Components of the Treatment

The MBCT-Dual treatment program for adolescents includes the following components:

Initial and Ongoing Assessment

The first step is to introduce the therapy and obtain the adolescent's and parents' (or guardians') agreement to participate. We recommend that treatment begin with a comprehensive evaluation that assesses the severity of the adolescent's PTSD symptoms, substance abuse, depression, and other emotional or behavioral problems as well as level of functioning across peer, family, and academic realms. Several reliable and valid tools can be obtained to assess common adolescent disorders including depression, anxiety, and ADHD. Recommended PTSD and addiction measures include the Child PTSD Symptom Scale (Foa, Ehlers, Clark, Tolin, & Orsillo, 1999) and the Teen Addiction Severity Index (Kaminer, Bukstein, & Tarter, 1991), both of which have been validated for use with adolescents and are readily available and relatively easy to use. Other useful measures include the Perceived Self-Compassion Scale (Neff, 2003), which helps to detect changes in compassion toward self and others from the beginning to the end of the therapy, and the Mindful Attention Awareness Scale for Adolescents (Black, Sussman, Johnson, & Milam, 2012). In addition, a referral for a psychiatric evaluation to assess the need for psychopharmacological treatment may be provided as needed.

At the start of treatment, you should assist the parents or guardians and the adolescent in preparing a list of signs that would indicate clinical deterioration (e.g., self-injury, violence, increased severity of mental health symptoms and/or substance abuse). Inform the family that if the adolescent begins to show these signs, they should contact you for assistance. The client may need a more intensive form of therapy such as inpatient substance abuse or psychiatric treatment if suicidal or homicidal ideation is indicated, if severe and potentially dangerous behaviors occur, or if functioning is significantly diminished.

Throughout treatment, it is important for you to monitor the adolescent's functioning for signs of clinical deterioration. Completing the Weekly Rating Sheet (see chapter 7) will allow you to monitor symptoms and help the adolescent review his or her goals and progress within therapy.

Motivational Interviewing

The motivational interviewing (MI) approach is based on the stages of change theory and the idea that people are often ambivalent about making changes (Miller & Johnson, 2001; Rollnick, Butler, Kinnersley, Gregory, & Mash, 2010; Waldron, Kern-Jones, Turner, Peterson, & Ozechowski, 2007). The premise of MI is that individuals, including adolescents, will be best able to engage in treatment and achieve change when their motivation is internally driven rather than imposed by the therapist. This is consistent with the mindfulness view that lasting change can only come from within. One specific MI approach, motivational enhancement, is a counseling technique that helps individuals resolve their ambivalence about engaging in treatment and ceasing their drug use. Motivational enhancement and other MI approaches are used in the introductory sessions to prepare adolescents for treatment, but they can also be helpful throughout the therapy's course. We recommend these approaches when eliciting the adolescent's story; asking about his or her concerns and hopes about treatment; evoking behavioral change; and addressing practical, psychological, and cultural barriers to treatment engagement such as stigma and mistrust of authority.

Psychoeducation

Psychoeducation facilitates the understanding, framing, and articulating of what one is experiencing—an important step in healing. In this phase of therapy, adolescents are informed about the neuroplasticity of the brain (its ability to adapt and heal), common reactions to trauma, and PTSD and its connection with substance use. This informational component uses visual elements and easily understood language rather than abstract terminology that often can be misinterpreted. Through education about PTSD symptoms and related problems, adolescents will be better able to understand their own reactions and the connections between their traumatic experiences, substance use, and other risky behaviors.

Cognitive Restructuring

CR involves learning to identify and then reframe thoughts and beliefs that contribute to distress by exploring them from a grounded and safe place. Adolescents learn to use self-monitoring to increase their awareness of these thoughts and beliefs and to identify patterns in their thinking that contribute to negative feelings, anxiety, depression, and risky behaviors such as drug use in their daily lives. Here adolescents also learn about drug and alcohol use triggers, the steps to recovery, and relapse prevention mechanisms—including awareness of early warning signs, identification of triggers and thoughts that lead to relapse, and strategies for being mindful of triggers and emotional responses to stress.

In this manual we use the five steps of CR: describing an upsetting situation, identifying the feelings associated with that situation, identifying the related underlying thought, evaluating the evidence for and against the upsetting thought, and changing the inaccurate thought (or making a plan to deal with the stress-inducing situation when the thought is accurate and a behavioral change may be in order).

CR works well with mindfulness practices to help adolescents bring awareness to thoughts and emotions while noticing and experiencing their impermanence. Along with a supportive clinician-adolescent relationship, CR is a central part of the treatment for core PTSD symptoms and addictions.

Mindfulness Practice

As the name of the program indicates, central to this treatment approach is the cultivation of mindfulness practices in adolescents who are dealing with issues of trauma and substance abuse. Mindfulness helps adolescents respond differently to addictions and compulsive behaviors by enabling them to become aware of the early warning signs, choose to orient their attention to the field of sounds or any other object of attention, and accept discomfort. In essence, mindfulness is "a process of learning to trust and stay with feelings of discomfort rather than trying to escape from or analyze them" (Stahl & Goldstein, 2010, p. 116).

By practicing mindfulness, adolescents develop the capacity to separate feeling from thinking and to see that thoughts come and go and are not necessarily true. Indeed, they learn that they are much larger than their thoughts. Thoughts are viewed as mere units in the field of awareness, just like sounds that appear, stay for a while, and then disappear.

Cultivating mindfulness helps adolescents with PTSD to cope with the spontaneous reexperiencing of the original traumatic event, which can present as flashbacks, involuntary movement, nightmares, and behavioral reenactment. By bringing awareness to what is happening from a witness stance, the person is not carried by the emotional current, and thus overall well-being improves.

Family Involvement

A supportive adult such as a parent can encourage the adolescent's participation and facilitate acquisition and maintenance of skills during and especially after treatment. A contraindication to including a parent, however, would be a history of offense, such as sexual or physical abuse, by the adult toward the adolescent. In cases of intergenerational trauma, use clinical judgment in weighing whether or not participation by the parent would be appropriate. If the parent also has mental health concerns, it may be advisable to refer him or her to treatment as well. In addition to providing informed consent, parental (or guardian) participation will likely involve, at minimum, attending an initial meeting to learn about the therapy, and for greater benefit, attending a session to jointly practice mindful communication within the parent-child dyad (chapter 5). However, it is extremely important to discuss with the adolescent any proposed involvement by an adult. Limits of confidentiality—which generally involve child abuse, imminent risk to self or others, and life-threatening situations—should be addressed and clarified early. Short of life-threatening situations, you should generally include the adolescent in conversations with parents about risky situations (e.g., the adolescent smoking more marijuana) that warrant safety considerations. The simple disclosure by the adolescent of alcohol or drug use does not automatically warrant disclosure to parents.

Bringing It All Together: Mindfulness-Based Cognitive Therapy for Adolescents

MBCT-Dual brings together mindfulness and CT. A common question is whether these approaches are compatible or are at cross-purposes, but as you will see, they are not only compatible but also complementary. While CT can help adolescents identify and modify unrealistic thoughts and beliefs and to consider—and ultimately adopt—new behaviors, combining it with mindfulness training can help them learn to develop awareness of the processes that maintain the unrealistic thoughts and beliefs to begin with. That is, the combination of mindfulness and CT helps change the process of thinking, not just the content of thoughts.

Mindfulness is the capacity to observe the thoughts that appear in the field of our mind without trying to ignore them or push them away—tactics that accomplish the opposite of what we desire. It is easy to get trapped in the content of the thought and begin to "unpack" it, readily moving into the past or future. With mindfulness we are invited to be present to the thoughts that emerge, to observe keenly the arising, the maintaining, and the dissolving of the thought. When we do that we can see clearly that thoughts are impermanent, just like clouds.

When we are aware of disallowing ourselves to be trapped in the content of the thought, the thought changes and dissolves spontaneously. Thoughts with a high emotional charge tend to hook our attention and lead us to contrive stories that may be untrue. MBCT-Dual allows the adolescent to become aware of his or her thoughts and feelings and become "unhooked" from those narratives that cause distress and unproductive behaviors.

When practicing mindfulness we do not try to ignore negative thoughts or to stop ourselves from thinking (Tan, 2012). We simply allow ourselves to observe as clearly as we can what we are thinking and feeling and to differentiate our thoughts from our feelings. We witness the thoughts from a grounded place by being aware of the breath, sensations in the body, or any of the five senses to keep us rooted in present moment awareness (Santorelli, 1999). By remaining in this state we can reduce the tendency of the mind to exaggerate negative emotions, thereby diminishing feelings of guilt, shame, blame, fear, and criticism of ourselves and others.

Thoughts, emotions, and sensations are like the waves on the ocean. They start, reach a peak, and slowly recede. In regards to facing difficulties in life, a favorite phrase from Jon Kabat-Zinn, originally by Swami Satichidananda, is "You can't stop the waves, but you can learn to surf" (Goldstein & Kornfield, 1987, p. 64). When we begin to pay attention to how our mind works, we notice that it constantly moves into the past—to memories, regrets, blame, guilt, or shame—or it goes to the future with "what if" questions, creating fear. If at times it is particularly difficult to let go of a thought or emotion because of a strong attachment or emotional valence, we can become interested in the sensations produced by clinging to the thought or emotion, getting to know the thought or emotion intimately, and noticing the consequences in our mind and body of holding on to it. Then, if possible, we can return our awareness to the breath or any of the five senses, bringing our attention to present moment awareness.

Danny: A Case Study of How Things Come Together

Danny is a sixteen-year-old boy who emigrated from Honduras to the United States with his aunt when he was fourteen years old. He had experienced many violent and gang-related events, and he himself was stabbed when he was thirteen years old. During the psychoeducation exercises, the therapist asked him about his understanding of how he was affected by these events in his life. He shared that he had recurring memories of being attacked and was also sad about the poverty and hunger his family in Honduras were still enduring.

Since moving to the United States, Danny sometimes became sick to his stomach when he ate, and at times he even vomited. He also had frequent nightmares. He had taken to smoking cannabis to calm his constant worry and anxiety.

The therapist reflected back what she heard about Danny's concern for his family back home. Through the course of therapy Danny began to notice the waves of sadness he experienced and the regret and shame he felt for being in the United States without his parents and younger sister and brother, as he believed he had left them behind to be hungry. He noticed that these thoughts were sometimes making him feel sick when he ate.

With the help of his therapist, Danny explored how his worries were a trigger for anxiety and depression and considered the positive ways he might act on behalf of his family in Honduras, for example, praying for them or studying and working toward getting a job to be able to help them. Danny used mindfulness practices to focus on his feelings and his reactions in the moment and became more and more aware of his thoughts

> and feelings—both emotional and physical. He learned to explore these sensations and feelings more compassionately, and he became less anxious as well as more open to responding in new ways to his situation and that of his family. Consequently, cannabis became less necessary for managing his feelings.

As seen in Danny's case, CT and mindfulness practices integrate successfully to diminish negative sequelae of trauma, build awareness for responding in new ways, and aid in recovery. In the next chapter, we will consider more specifically the theory and practice of MBCT-Dual.

Chapter 2

Theory and Practice of Mindfulness-Based Cognitive Therapy–Dual

Most people spend their entire life imprisoned within the confines of their own thoughts. They never go beyond a narrow, mind-made, personalized sense of self that is conditioned by the past.

—Eckhart Tolle

This manual is part of a growing body of practices that combine the approaches found in CT and mindfulness. Aaron T. Beck developed CT for the treatment of depression in 1979 (Beck, Rush, Shaw, & Emery, 1979). Beck became interested in how unconscious and automatic thoughts can influence, trigger, and perpetuate distressing feelings in depressed patients. A central aim of CT is to impart skills that assist the individual in taking note of these automatic thoughts and the ways that they impact feelings and actions. CT provides a tool for reframing these thoughts. Clients are introduced to the cognitive model: thinking influences emotion, body sensations, and behavior. By becoming aware of negative, unhelpful thought patterns when they are occurring, it is possible to modify them and overcome automatic reactions and feelings.

The MBCT-Dual intervention has, as its name indicates, mindfulness at the center. Mindfulness meditation is grounded in Buddhist philosophy, which has existed for over 2,500 years. Mindfulness as a secular intervention started with the specific aim of helping patients with chronic pain. CT and mindfulness would seem to be quite different, perhaps even incompatible. In fact, meditation practitioners as well as those with a western psychological science orientation originally expressed concerns about this partnership. Some meditation practitioners have argued that mindfulness-based interventions have been watered down and do not have the ethical grounding that comes with the practice of more comprehensive Buddhist principles. On the other hand, those with a psychological science perspective have expressed concern that an approach based not on rationality but on ingredients such as loving-kindness and compassion is not easily measurable. This has changed in the last few years. Evidence-based studies in loving-kindness and compassion conducted by Hofman, Sawyer, Witt, and Oh (2010), Germer (2009), Neff (2011), and Garrison, Scheinost, Constable, and Brewer (2014) have been able to show the neural impact of compassion and loving-kindness using neuroimaging.

Indeed, the marriage between CT and mindfulness has borne much fruit. MBCT for depression has proven to be successful with patients who have experienced three or more depressive episodes, and the evidence is supported by controlled outcome trials and other research (Godfrin & van Heeringen, 2010; Kuyken et al., 2010; Teasdale et al., 2000). These studies show that MBCT reduces depression relapse probability in the year following treatment by about 50 percent compared to typical treatment (e.g., antidepressant medication). MBCT has also been used in large-scale trials with patients who are actively depressed (Barnhofer & Chittka, 2009), showing beneficial results. In 2010, Segal et al. published the results of a randomized controlled trial demonstrating that MBCT for depression is as effective as antidepressants (Segal et al., 2010).

Furthermore, similar to CT, mindfulness holds that unconscious and automatic thoughts can influence, trigger, and perpetuate distressing and limiting feelings. Mindfulness in turn allows one to become balanced and grounded in the body while taking note of these automatic thoughts and the ways that they impact feelings, body sensations, and ultimately behavior. Mindfulness provides awareness of the constricting nature of the mind and the body when one is faced with difficulty. By seeing clearly the tunnel vision that arises with traumatic events and difficulties, the choice to reframe is made even more possible. Awareness influences thinking, emotions, bodily sensations, perceptions, moods, and behavior. The belief in mindfulness is that effortless transformation happens just by being present and aware. By becoming aware of negative, unhelpful thought patterns when they are occurring, it is possible to see them for what they are, and from there to allow them to flow out of awareness without having to act on or be emotionally captured by them. Table 2.1 shows a comparison of CT and mindfulness principles and how these complement one another in MBCT for treating depression, trauma, and substance-use disorders.

Table 2.1 Comparison of Cognitive Therapy, Mindfulness, and MBCT

Cognitive Therapy	Mindfulness	MBCT
Has a goal-oriented approach.	Promotes openness to unexpected outcomes.	Has a goal-oriented approach and promotes openness to unexpected outcomes.
Encourages experimenting with alternative behaviors instead of maintaining maladaptive behaviors that stem from distorted thinking.	Fosters a new way of being—an openness to what unfolds moment-to-moment and to the boundless internal resources available to heal and change.	Leads one to pay attention to the early warning signs of an impending relapse and to build one's capacity to respond.
Shows how by identifying negative, unhelpful thought patterns as they occur, one can modify them and overcome automatic reactions and feelings.	Fosters awareness of thoughts, emotions, and bodily sensations so choice is possible through clear seeing. Provides a safe space for what is important to emerge and helps make the unconscious conscious through inquiry.	Invites one to be aware of where the mind is orienting and, by seeing clearly, to redirect it to more useful and supportive thoughts.
Encourages challenging and changing automatic thoughts and distorted patterns of thinking.	Brings to awareness habitual tendencies of the mind and allows the possibility of choosing differently.	Facilitates transformation through commitment, intention to redirect thoughts, and the use of mindfulness tools to "come back to balance."
Encourages identifying and analyzing automatic thoughts and patterns of distorted thinking.	Encourages awareness of automatic thoughts and curiosity regarding negative or disturbing thoughts. Invites one to take a step back, notice the thought with curiosity, feel the effects without taking action, observe it fade from awareness, and be comfortable with "a not-knowing mind."	Invites one to pay attention to the thoughts that attempt to control people, places, and things; notice the impulse to act on them; and try to bring spaciousness and alternatives to those thoughts.
Encourages changing maladaptive patterns of thoughts and behaviors.	Encourages paying attention to maladaptive thoughts and behaviors with a sense of exploration and kindness. Prompts one to accept the way things are at a particular moment, be proactive, and choose more skillfully.	Fosters deep motivation to change, with self-compassion and acceptance to avoid relapse.

Using MBCT-Dual

MBCT-Dual uses CT techniques to help adolescents with PTSD and addictions become aware of negative thought patterns when they are occurring and choose how to respond instead of succumbing to the automatic reactions and feelings that tend to control behavior. It employs mindfulness as a practice for building awareness; cultivating affectionate curiosity; and befriending the thoughts, emotions, and bodily sensations that arise moment-to-moment, without unpacking their content or taking the usual stance of avoidance and pursuit.

PTSD often co-occurs with other mental health conditions, most commonly depression, anxiety, and addictions. With every relapse into addiction or depression, it becomes harder to pull out of a vicious cycle that potentially traps the person for decades or a lifetime. Adolescents, with youth on their side, have an opportunity to learn practices and coping skills that can help divert this cycle. Mindfulness allows the person to observe the early warning signs of PTSD symptoms, addictive cravings and urges, and depressive moods. By observing clearly what is happening in the internal landscape (composed of thoughts, emotions, bodily sensations, perceptions, moods, and mind narratives), skillful choices can be made to prevent the activation, escalation, or reinforcement of dangerous, self-destructive states or patterns. Instead of reacting in habitual and automatic ways, adolescents who practice mindfulness can learn to respond differently and not allow avoidance or self-defeating thoughts or actions to rule their lives.

A mindfulness-based approach invites acceptance of what is arising moment-to-moment whether we like it or not. It allows for kindness, patience, and compassion toward ourselves and all that exists. It helps us let go of our attachment to our views and any goals that we are holding dear, making room for all that arises inwardly, instead of pushing, ignoring, changing, denying, or trying to conquer thoughts and emotions. It offers awareness of the body (breath, sensations, and the five senses) and the mind. It invites participants to have intimate knowledge of the ingredients that make something pleasant, neutral, or unpleasant for them; to intimately know the feeling tone, or signature in the body, of those states; and, if desired, to be able to respond differently.

Whereas CT primarily involves challenging thoughts, mindfulness practices invite participants to observe a thought and let it flow through the mind, without getting trapped in its content. Participants are invited to experience the direct sensations that arise in the body when a particular thought pattern is activated. They are invited to observe not only the pain that cannot be avoided but also the "extra" discomfort caused by resisting, wanting things to be different, or fabricating stories of how things should be. They are invited to observe the impermanence of thoughts, emotions, sensations, cravings, and urges. Finally, they are given an opportunity to expand and reframe how things are understood and experienced.

What Are the Intentions of MBCT-Dual?

As you prepare to use this therapy model with adolescents, it is important to keep these specific goals for the client in mind:

- Learning to use mindfulness meditation practices to reduce PTSD, depression, and co-occurring substance-use problems.
- Increasing awareness of present, moment-to-moment experiences.
- Recognizing when, in everyday life, negative emotions and reactions trigger a doing mode, and learning how to disengage from that mode and enter into a being mode.
- Developing additional coping strategies, such as cognitive reframing, and techniques to respond effectively to negative thoughts, emotions, cravings, and urges.
- Integrating these skills through continued mindfulness practice to stay well, befriend oneself, prevent future relapse, and promote recovery.
- Practicing how to inhabit the body instead of living in the mind.
- Experiencing the body and mind with neutrality, curiosity, and openness.

You will see that the treatment sessions involve practicing and developing these overarching skills, building on each component through the course of therapy, and inviting the adolescent to use these skills and approaches in everyday life.

Cultivating Reframing to Cope Effectively with Difficulties

Reframing is a key concept in mindfulness and MBCT-Dual. Cognitive reframing refers to almost any conscious shift—positive or negative—in a person's mental perspective or mindset. It is simply seeing more than what is inside our usual perceptions. It is appreciating how the parts relate to the whole. It is moving out of a confined and separate appreciation of a situation into a more expansive and holistic view. It is asking oneself: *Am I seeing the entirety of this situation, or have I been caught in a few aspects of what is happening?* This is similar to taking a photo in a "wide-angle" rather than a "zooming" view.

Restructuring, on the other hand, is the act of therapeutically changing one's mindset to strengthen oneself; therefore, it always has a positive connotation and is more goal oriented. In MBCT-Dual we are asking the adolescent to intentionally see a more holistic and expansive view of a thought as related to a given situation. In the end, a more compassionate or positive interpretation may emerge through restructuring. But the reframing—seeing more than we did initially—is a worthwhile first step.

The Nine Dots Exercise helps adolescents gain an understanding of reframing. This is a puzzle in which nine dots are arranged in a square formation with three dots per row, as shown below:

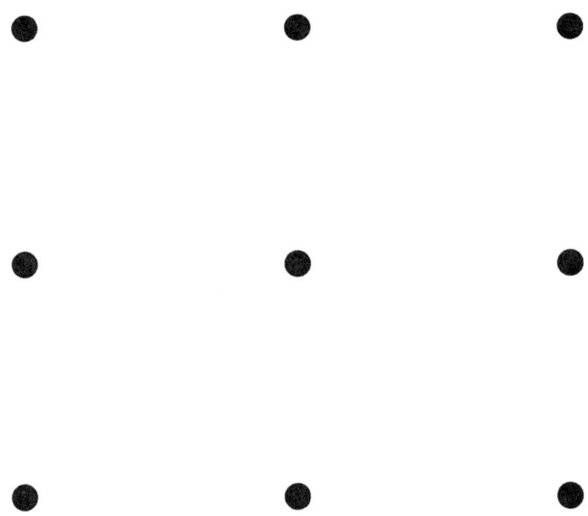

The participant is invited to connect all the dots by making four straight lines, without lifting the pencil or retracing any line. The aim of this age-old exercise is not necessarily to solve the problem but to observe clearly the emotions, thoughts, physical sensations, beliefs, and habitual patterns that surface in the process of solving the puzzle. Often people find the exercise extremely frustrating, and they feel incompetent if they cannot solve it or if they once knew how but forgot. Habitual patterns emerge, such as giving up after trying a few times, asking others to do it, "googling" the answer, persisting until exhaustion, or not being able to sleep due to preoccupation with how to solve it. Some people become aware of an inner narrative that is blaming, abusive, attacking, and self-defeating: *You are stupid; you cannot solve anything in your life, not even this small problem that was given to you*; or *You are inadequate*. There is usually an "aha" experience when the person sees the way it is done. (Hint: To solve the problem you have to move your line outside of the perceived box formed by the dots.)

Why can it be so challenging to solve this problem? Most people tend to see the nine-dot square pattern as the field of the problem instead of considering the whole page or board as the field to work with, sometimes spending an inordinate amount of time and energy on an approach that will never allow them to accomplish what they want. This simple exercise can translate to everyday life; that is, people often put their energy and efforts into solving only small parts of their difficult situation, leaving out what is really important and being unable to see the bigger picture outside of a constrained "box." Usually when faced with difficulty, our minds tend to contract and see only certain angles of the situation, so we concentrate on solving the problem in that circumscribed, limited way. The inability to solve something (that cannot possibly be solved within that parameter) may generate strong feelings of frustration and discomfort, which in turn might lead to drug use or other actions that worsen the situation. When we become mindful of our inner narratives and beliefs, we can observe this tendency to limit and create boundaries for ourselves, which, after some time, we begin to believe are unmovable and true.

A systems perspective, which is developed through mindfulness practice, invites us to expand our awareness and to work with the entire field, or the wholeness, of the situation. We need to understand the totality of the problem and how the various parts relate to it as a whole. Unless we are able to see the whole picture and assess the situation in its entirety, we will never be able to find a long-term solution. To solve our pressing problems, we first have to develop the ability to reframe or expand our thinking to consider not only the immediate, isolated part we are seeing but also the part that we are not seeing due to habitual patterns that may not incorporate new information or the totality of the situation. It is important to appreciate that how and what we see or don't see in a situation will affect the way we think, feel, and behave.

Mindfully Being

As human beings, we have many methods for avoiding emotional discomfort: distracting ourselves, obsessing, ruminating, eating, drinking alcohol, or taking drugs. Avoidance works in the short term, but the next time difficult thoughts or emotions arise, we are in the same place as the last time: feeling disturbed and criticizing ourselves for not being good enough, for being too weak, or for making mistakes.

The being mode, described earlier, is a healthier way of interacting with our experiences and cultivates the conditions for mindfulness. Rather than thinking about our experience, we are actually in it, as it really is. For example, check in right now: What body sensations are you experiencing in this present moment? What are the thoughts hanging around? What emotions, if any, are present?

In being mode we get to see how things change, both the pleasant and the unpleasant. Once we see this, the impermanence of our thoughts and moods becomes our friend, and we can create some space from feeling "tied up in knots."

Why bother? Sometimes, if we don't resist our experience—being in a miserable mood, complaining to ourselves, wishing things were different—awareness and acceptance emerge. Then, something opens up, and there is a taste of freedom.

Earlier we discussed the goals of MBCT-Dual: offering practices and approaches that assist an individual in being more present in the moment, more embodied, more aware, and more responsive rather than reactive. There are six key concepts and practices that assist in building awareness of how the mind works and moving us from the doing mode to the being mode:

1. **Being aware of automatic pilot.** The formal and informal practice of mindfulness helps us recognize our tendency to be on automatic pilot—that is, to experience automatic and repetitive thoughts and reactions without awareness. Mindfulness practices illuminate the chatter of the mind and how it tends to control our reactions to everyday events. Practices such as the body scan help adolescents learn to focus on what they sense in specific areas and throughout their body, revealing how we are often unaware of what we are experiencing and can fall back into automatic pilot mode.

2. **Practicing mindfulness of the breath or sounds.** With a greater awareness of how the mind can be busy and scattered, adolescents begin to concentrate better. Participants learn to intentionally focus on the breath or sounds as an aid to skillfully "ride the waves" of discomfort, cravings, aversions, and attachments.

3. **Staying present.** Adolescents develop the ability to stay focused on the moment, sense what is being experienced in that moment, and widen their perspective on how they relate to experiences both internally (body sensations, emotions, thoughts, perceptions) and in interactions with others.

4. **Dealing with mood shifts.** Participants learn to handle mood shifts by employing cognitive approaches as well as mindfulness strategies such as the STOP technique, which offers an opportunity to notice what is happening in one's body, emotions, or thoughts and to find equilibrium before acting or reacting (see chapter 7, meeting 5 for more details about this technique). The STOP technique helps to elicit a mindful response to stress.

5. **Awareness that thoughts are not facts.** This is central to cognitive theory as well as mindfulness. Participants learn to recognize thoughts as merely thoughts, not reality. Negative thoughts can restrict our ability to relate to experiences in different ways. The recognition that we can witness our thoughts, we are not our thoughts, and that thoughts are merely secretions of the mind that could be true or false offers us the opportunity to experience our lives and situations differently and more expansively.
6. **Employing self-care and compassion.** In MBCT-Dual, adolescents learn specific strategies to use when depression, anxiety, or relapse threatens. Each participant learns to identify his or her unique warning signs of relapse, respond to those signs compassionately, and seek help from others as needed.

Understanding these concepts helps adolescents with dual diagnosis to deal with future mood difficulties and relapse risks. If adolescents learn the techniques in this manual in the early stage of their substance use, it may avert the development of chronic and severe addictions. In cases where addictions have progressed, the integration of mindfulness and stress reduction approaches in MBCT-Dual can promote recovery and relapse prevention.

Five Steps of Cognitive Restructuring

Are our thoughts facts? This is a central question in MBCT-Dual, as in any mindfulness- and cognitive-based approach. The tendency to believe that our thoughts are the truth can be the cause of much suffering—especially when we are caught up in the negative cascading thoughts so common to depressed, anxious, or stressed states. It is during these times that our thoughts go around and around in our attempt to find solutions. This analytical mode—useful in so many other areas of our lives—is not so effective for dealing with emotional distress. Whenever there is a sense of *I have to* or *I should*, we can be pretty sure we are in this mode, the one we enter when we want things to be different. We try to figure out why we are feeling the way we are, we push the feelings away, or we avoid them.

In this manual you will see that the early sessions focus on building rapport and motivation, and right from the beginning mindfulness is introduced. The practice starts with simple mindful breathing. You will then move on to practicing mindfulness at the beginning of every session, building the capacity for both you and the adolescent to be fully present and aware during the sessions. Practice at home for both you and the client is encouraged; that includes formal meditations as well as informal practices such as mindful eating and mindful walking.

The five steps of cognitive restructuring, outlined below, build on this mindful awareness through the use of cognitive therapy techniques:

Step 1: The situation. Identify and write down a situation which has emotional saliency or is notable to you; something experienced through the senses and related to thoughts, feelings, and bodily sensations evoked by that situation, as in these examples: You had to go to the store; you began to think that you were in danger, and you felt very anxious. You had an argument with someone, became aware of tension in your body, and had thoughts of being rejected. You had a vivid memory of a stressful event that evoked bodily sensations or thoughts (e.g., you felt your heart racing when you were walking down the street alone). Employ mindfulness practices to first become aware of the situation. Next, in steps 2 and 3, we will identify how you experience this situation in your body and your mind.

Step 2: The feeling. Identify and name the uncomfortable feeling related to the situation. It could be:

- fear
- anxiety/stress
- sadness/depression
- guilt/shame
- anger
- any other emotion

Step 3: The thought. Identify the thoughts around the situation as specifically as possible, because general thoughts are more difficult to examine or reframe. Look at these thoughts with curiosity and self-compassion. Below are some examples of thoughts that lend themselves to exploration and reframing:

- I am a bad person because I argued with my friend.
- I will never be okay because of the abuse that happened to me.
- I will never make it to college because I flunked my exam.
- I can't trust anyone because I will always be hurt by people.
- If I don't use drugs, I will not be able to deal.

Step 4: Examine the thought. Explore that thought with as much openness and intention as possible, from all angles: *How do I feel thinking that? How does my body feel? Are there other thoughts attached to that? How do I feel about holding* *on to that thought? Do I want to hold on to it tightly? Do I want to let go of it? Do I want this at all? How do I treat myself when I have this thought? How do I treat others?*

Examine how true the thought is or how much "weight" it holds by considering all available evidence for and against it.

Step 5: Action plan. If the evidence does support your thought, create a plan of action to respond to the situation or to the effects of the automatic thought and your impulse to react. Is there something you can do to remind yourself of the other possibilities? Is there a mantra you need to remember? How could your mindfulness practice help? Do you need support from a trusted friend? Do you need added safety for yourself in this situation? Do you need to ride the roller coaster of the emotions (explained later in this chapter) that come with that thought so that it, too, can pass? Consider all of these possibilities and available options.

Case Examples

The following two examples illustrate the use and benefits of thought identification and reframing strategies:

Jerry

Jerry is a fifteen-year-old African American male who witnessed his best friend drown after falling into turbulent water. Jerry exhibited ongoing feelings of anger, guilt, and sadness about the event. He felt he should have been strong enough to jump in and save his friend, but others who were present during the tragedy had stopped him to prevent him from also drowning. Jerry lived in an environment where physical strength and toughness are important; he felt he should have used this strength to save his friend and that his failure to do so was the cause of his friend's drowning and death.

Using CR, Jerry was able to assess the validity of the thought that his friend died because he had not been strong enough to save him. Statements verifying the thought included (1) Jerry is physically strong enough to save someone and (2) he could have jumped in. Alternative statements included (1) his friend fell into a dangerous area that would have put them both at risk, (2) Jerry was not a good swimmer himself, (3) he had been held back from jumping in by people who were concerned and scared, and (4) he loved his friend and would have saved him if he could have. Eventually, rather than continuing to focus on guilt, Jerry came to express his sadness, describing how tense he felt in his body every time he thought about the event. In future therapy meetings he went on to share past situations in which his father was verbally abusive and made him feel useless. Using CR, he reframed thoughts related to his self-worth. He also began to reflect upon how his anger toward his father was often triggered whenever he was challenged by other males. He used mindfulness practices to build better awareness of his emotional and physical reactions to these situations and to come back to the awareness of his own breath to ground himself in the present whenever he became angry or anxious. This helped reduce his tendency to move into thoughts and patterns related to his past trauma and allowed him to adjust his automatic reactions.

Later, Jerry used the STOP technique to become more aware of his thoughts and reactions in situations where he felt triggered to react angrily. He learned to stop and note what he was feeling, pause, and find balance before acting. This also became useful when his impulse was to drink alcohol or smoke weed.

Jerry developed an action plan to explore other ways to use his physical strength. He aimed to become a strong swimmer and help younger kids learn how to swim, as he noted that a lot of African American kids in his neighborhood did not know how to swim and were therefore in danger of drowning. Over time he was able to rate his sense of personal guilt for his friend's death as less intense.

Being aware of his self-narrative, Jerry learned to be more compassionate toward himself, to not attack himself so harshly, and to have patience with ingrained habitual patterns that kept showing up despite his efforts to change.

Amanda

Amanda is a seventeen-year-old Latina female who was sexually abused by her uncle between the ages of seven and ten. She worked on mindfulness practices with her therapist for a few weeks, becoming aware of pleasant and unpleasant feelings. She began to notice some thoughts and physical reactions regarding her sexuality. She shared with the therapist that she thought she was "damaged goods" and felt as though she was a bad person every time she thought about sex or was attracted to someone.

To reframe and weigh the evidence for her thought that she was a bad person for having sexual feelings, Amanda offered and considered the following statements with help from her therapist: (1) "When I think about sexual thoughts, I feel strange in the center of my body and feel as if there is something wrong with me"; (2) "Sexual feeling have always been about bad things for me"; (3) "When I have had sexual experiences [the sexual abuse] in the past, only bad things have come from it"; and (4) "My family was angry at me for having dishonored them when I disclosed my abuse."

The evidence she was able to consider that did not support the thought included (1) "I was young and did not ask for or consent to having sex with an adult"; (2) "It is different when I feel attracted to someone my age"; and (3) "Sexual feelings are normal, so my sexual feelings are normal, I guess." Amanda expressed that she still held on to the original thought that there is something wrong with her sexual feelings, but she agreed that maybe she is not a bad person—she just became confused as a result of the sexual abuse she experienced as a child.

Amanda made an action plan to let herself explore relationships with boys that did not involve sex to see how she could be safe and how age-appropriate relationships could feel different than the sexual abuse she had endured. She agreed to explore some of the wide range of feelings she could possibly experience. She was open to the outcome. She used these insights to build an awareness of how she sometimes used drugs and alcohol to avoid feelings she believed were negative and came to understand that these behaviors only reinforced thoughts that she was a bad person.

Before treatment Amanda experienced her PTSD symptoms in a psychosomatic way. She tended to have severe stomach cramping and dizziness whenever her PTSD was triggered. Through therapy, she began to use mindfulness practices such as brief body scans to become more aware of her automatic thoughts and physical reactions so that she could respond with CR, mindfulness breathing, or engagement in her action plan.

Riding the Roller Coaster of Emotions

MBCT-Dual uses mindfulness practices and cognitive techniques to help adolescents identify and respond differently to substance-use triggers and cravings. Riding the Roller Coaster of Emotions (see appendix A) is a helpful exercise to address addiction-related feelings and behaviors. It is adapted from the Urge Surfing exercise presented in *Mindfulness-Based Relapse Prevention for Addictive Behaviors,* by Sarah Bowen, Neha Chawla, and G. Alan Marlatt (2011).

In Urge Surfing, participants are asked to picture the urge as an ocean wave and imagine surfing, using their breath as a surfboard to ride the wave. They ride the wave of craving through its peak and its decline, without being submerged or wiped out by its intensity. In the roller coaster version, the adolescent is asked to notice the ups and downs, the turns and shifts that can occur with emotions, and to ride these feelings with awareness.

The purpose of this exercise is to learn to connect with the experience of cravings and urges with affectionate curiosity. This kind of curiosity is compassionate, nonjudgmental, gentle, and at the same time focused. In MBCT-Dual, affectionate curiosity is offered as a specific way to use mindfulness skills. The aim is to try to see with clarity what is driving one's feelings—what is below the surface and at the root of the craving. Is the desire to use substances due to disturbing emotions or happy emotions, the need to fit in among peers, the need for liberation, or simply to try something different, exciting, and risky?

The first step is to bring to the mind's eye a challenging experience, to see it as clearly as possible: where, with whom, how, what? Once that is clear, the invitation is to notice, as best as possible, the bodily sensations, emotions, feelings, and thoughts that arise—not to change anything, but just to see clearly.

Sometimes the body scan, for which two guided meditations are offered in appendix A, is used as a model. The detailed nature of the body scan serves effectively in the process of seeing: paying attention to the sensations in the big toe, the little toe, the toes in between, the spaces between the toes, the sensations of temperature or moisture in the skin, and so on.

Rather than falling into the usual pattern of reacting or resisting, the intention here is to become intimate with what arises when cravings or urges are present by asking and answering a series of questions: Where do you feel it in your body? Can you observe the rise and fall (undulating nature) of cravings and urges—appearing, moving upward and reaching a peak, and then falling or subsiding? What do you say to yourself when you have been captured by an urge or a craving? Can you observe the thoughts that are connected to this feeling? Do you recognize thoughts of anticipation or desperation (*I cannot stand it one more moment; I am going to fall apart; this experience will be too much for me*)? What emotions are present? Can you feel the intensity and where the particular emotions are felt? How do you treat yourself and how do you treat others when you have an urge or craving?

Jake

Jake smoked marijuana so that he could relax and focus better. However, he felt motivated to stop because he started to cough a lot during sports activities. Using the body scan meditation, he noticed that when he craved smoking, that craving lasted only a few short minutes. He experimented with seeing how long it lasted and whether he could ride the wave of that craving. He noticed that his cravings came not only when he felt anxious but also when he felt joyful. He realized that he had thought he could not do things well without smoking, so he tested that out, too, with some curiosity. He smoked less and less.

Mary

Mary drank alcohol to enhance her mood. She often felt depressed and could not let go of the sadness without drinking. She had fun with her peers when she drank, but she sometimes ended up having unprotected sex when intoxicated, and that worried her. She was open to finding ways to deal with her mood without relying on alcohol. She learned to do mindful breathing to bring herself to the present moment and began to notice the negative thoughts she often had about herself—for example, *You are worthless*. With the help of her clinician she began to wonder about why she had that thought, and she also noticed her automatic reactions, which included wanting to drink. She experimented with alternative ways of seeing herself and the situations she often found herself in. She considered activities to do other than drinking. She took action about being safer and being with safer people. With guidance, she was open to seeing what might happen differently if she made other choices, such as going out with a good friend to the movies. With self-compassion, she worked on identifying and changing her thoughts that were associated with sadness, anger, and regret.

As these cases illustrate, in this space of awareness adolescents are encouraged to consider common thought patterns related to using drugs and alcohol. To facilitate this, invite them to once again ask themselves: what are some alternative thoughts or ways of seeing these things? Even if they are not convinced they need to change anything, they can keep track of their triggers for substance use in a diary and discuss these triggers in sessions to continue to discover coping strategies. Encourage adolescents to consider their own ideas for strategies or changes that can help them in specific situations to avoid drug or alcohol use. If there are people who lead them to use drugs when they don't want to, you can role-play and help them practice how to say no. If they drink to relax and cope with stress, they can consider alternative ways to achieve this outcome. The more the adolescents can offer their own suggestions and ideas, the more likely they will be successful.

Stress Reduction and Overcoming Adversity

As trauma is a central issue you will address using MBCT-Dual, understanding the physiological impact of trauma as well as the critical role of resiliency in the adolescents you treat will augment the effectiveness of your work. What follows is a basic background of how trauma affects the body and mind and how this connects to the practices you will engage in with the adolescents you treat (Schouela, 2014).

The Polyvagal Theory and Chronic Trauma

Until recently, it was believed that organisms have only two inherent defensive systems. One is the sympathetic nervous system, which functions as an arousal system. Its task is to mobilize and hasten action through the fight-or-flight reaction. It increases metabolic and cardiac activity, acting as an accelerator of emotions and physical sensations. The other defense system is the parasympathetic nervous system; it has the function of regulating and calming nervous system activity. It acts as a brake in modulating emotions and helps to renew and restore stability. This system evolved about three hundred million years ago.

This view was recently challenged by Porges (2009; Porges & Furman, 2011), who described three defensive systems instead of two. This third automatic reaction of the organism is known as the polyvagal theory.

Porges coined the word "neuroception," describing it as the unconscious, continuous assessment of risk. This defense system can quiet down the sympathetic pathways to the heart, activating the relational, or social, brain without our conscious awareness and fostering "approach" behavior, peacefulness, and balance when the organism feels safe. Conversely, and also without our conscious awareness, it can activate avoidance and shutdown—when it perceives internal risk (produced by our own disturbing thoughts and emotions) or external risk (produced by people, places, and things). According to Porges (2009), this third system evolved about five hundred million years ago and can be traced to early fish species. It originates in a primitive area of the brainstem known as the dorsal motor nucleus of the vagus.

The vagus is the largest nerve of the autonomic nervous system, with 80 percent of its fibers mapping our visceral experiences and communicating them to the brain. It can regulate cardiac output to foster engagement with or disengagement from the environment. It links the neural regulation of the heart to social behavior including responses to others' actions, affective experiences, emotional expressions, facial gestures, and vocal communication. The avoidance aspect of this system functions to preserve life by immobilization and energy conservation. It does this by inhibiting the breath, decreasing metabolic function and heart rate, and shutting down the reactive mobilizing system. However, when it perceives safety, it does the opposite: it calms and promotes restoration and health.

An important finding related to the polyvagal theory is that individuals with trauma histories have depressed cardiac vagal tone, which limits the ability to rapidly recover and to support a calm physiological state. According to Porges (2009; Porges & Furman, 2011), individuals with psychiatric disorders, including PTSD, experience longstanding difficulty regulating their emotional state and display, among other characteristics, defensive behaviors and a flatness of affective tone. Porges also states that in situations where a child is subjected to sexual or physical abuse, where the possibility of escaping is unlikely, a shutdown response is triggered. Levine and Mate (2010) affirmed Porges's theory and argued that those with a history of severe neglect or abuse are dominated by the immobilization or shutdown system; that is, in the face of stress the tendency is to become numb, paralyzed, and unable to make choices, and the heart rate either remains constant or decreases. Additionally, dissociative symptoms, depersonalization, gastrointestinal problems, migraines, chronic fatigue, chronic pain, and disengagement from life often occur.

The hallmark of childhood trauma is the taking away of choice. The child is put in a situation where there is no chance to fight or flee. Shutdown, feigned immobilization, and learned helplessness are initially adaptive coping strategies; over time, however, these strategies are no longer helpful yet continue to be unconsciously activated. Replacing these ineffective strategies with healthier responses must involve conscious choice. The antidote of having choice taken away is receiving choice back. Mindfulness propagates choice, fostering the possibility of healing from long-term trauma.

If adolescents who have been subjected to one-time or repeated trauma, neglect, or abuse are able to understand the neurobiological consequences of the abuse, they can learn to normalize what is happening to them. Instead of feeling defective or unworthy, they can adopt an attitude of self-compassion, kindness, and curiosity to observe as clearly as possible, moment-to-moment, what arises in the body, emotionally and cognitively.

Furthermore, adolescents with a history of trauma tend to feel disconnected from their bodies. They may not be able to feel their bodies and are often unaware of where their bodies begin or end in relation to others or to the space around them. The mindful movement and the body scan practices, intrinsic to MBCT-Dual, gently help to guide their awareness to the felt sense of their bodies, their muscles and joints, over and over again, creating new neural pathways of proprioception. By increasing body awareness, adolescents are able to make safe choices with their bodies based on what they actually feel. Gradually they learn that they have control over their bodies. For example, if they are experiencing discomfort in a particular yoga posture, they can learn that they have a choice to shift or adjust the form to offer themselves greater ease.

For adolescents who have experienced chronic early childhood trauma, the polyvagal theory has considerable salience. Repeated practice of mindfulness skills helps to activate the parasympathetic path in the autonomic nervous system, reducing the fight-or-flight reaction and the freeze response. It also produces increased vagal tone, which is associated with safety and positive relational experiences. In that regard there are some key functions that you, the clinician, serve in this process of mindfulness practice with the adolescent:

- Offering a safe space to guide the adolescent in learning and regularly practicing mindfulness with compassion, and conveying openness to the adolescent's preferences, process, and emerging insights.
- Offering a relationship and modeling compassion, curiosity, kindness, and nonjudgment during the very process in which the adolescent is developing awareness and insights.
- Trusting in the adolescent's emerging wisdom and offering a positive relational experience.
- Offering a space where you are mindfully present and responsive to the adolescent in the moment.

It is because you have the opportunity to offer these important elements that we reiterate how essential your personal practice of mindfulness is. Your own mindful presence is a crucial ingredient in the adolescent's path to healing.

Resiliency

MBCT-Dual is geared toward maintaining a mindfulness practice, fostering resiliency in the face of stress, overcoming adversity, and promoting recovery. It is important to define what is known as resiliency, or resilience: the capacity to recover quickly from difficulties. This is also known as "grit" or "stress hardiness." The Merriam-Webster dictionary defines "resilience" as the ability to become strong, healthy, or successful again after something bad happens (http://www.merriam-webster.com, s.v. "resilience"). In psychology, resilience is usually seen as an individual's ability to properly adapt to stress and adversity.

Suzanne Kobasa, a psychologist who coined the term "psychological hardiness," studied many groups of individuals performing stressful work. In every group she found individuals who were able to cope effectively and even thrive under stressful circumstances (Kobasa, 1979). She observed that there were three common characteristics in those who were happier and more resilient. The first was that they felt in control (rather than helpless) about what they were experiencing. They believed that they could exert some influence on the situation. It is important to note that this was their belief; it could have been true or untrue, but the fact that they believed that they were not at the mercy of whatever was unfolding was enough to increase their resiliency. The second characteristic was commitment. Stress-hardy people tend to be fully engaged in what they are doing and completely present in any interaction at work, home, or play. The last characteristic is challenge, which is defined as the ability to see difficulties as part of life (instead of threats), to "turn poison into medicine," and to learn and grow with every difficulty that arises.

Resiliency is learned. There are many factors that contribute to make someone resilient: optimism; positive thinking; problem-solving skills; the presence of a support system; and the ability to regulate emotions, to reframe, and to communicate. We address many of these in this manual. Some of these skills have been introduced in this chapter and will be practiced progressively during the course of the therapy sessions (outlined in detail in chapter 7). Our intention for the adolescents is that through their work with you, rather than letting failure and stressors overcome them and drain their resolve, they will find a way to rise from the ashes.

Chapter 3

Engaging, Motivating, and Working with Adolescents in Therapy

Life is a preparation for the future; and the best preparation for the future is to live as if there were none.

—Albert Einstein

Building a therapeutic alliance with adolescents early in treatment—although sometimes challenging—is essential. The literature on engaging adolescents in treatment has focused on three main areas: therapist behaviors that impede therapeutic relationship formation, relationship-enhancing engagement variables, and the role of parents. As a therapist who has practiced counseling with adolescents, you will likely have a strong sense of how to build a therapeutic alliance with young people. However, working with adolescents using a manual such as this one can feel challenging. Rigidly adhering to manuals, despite their proven effectiveness, can undermine the basis of forming an alliance, which is to tailor the therapeutic relationship to the individual needs and concerns of the client. The strict implementation of manuals can have implications for adolescent clients who may be less willing to develop an intimate relationship with a therapist; they may decline active participation in therapy that they perceive as uncollaborative and as adhering rigidly to an agenda rather than addressing their issues as they arise. Therapists who present themselves in an overly formal and didactic manner without acknowledging or showing understanding of the emotions and concerns that the adolescent raises have much greater difficulty engaging their clients in therapy than therapists who are warm, open, informal, and flexible.

CT strategies, including those presented in this book, can be delivered in a focused way for adolescents while still facilitating their engagement in therapy. Components that are at the heart of mindfulness—empathy, compassion, trust, positive regard, acceptance, and genuineness—have been linked to positive relationships with youth, increased participation in the therapeutic process, and improvement in clinical symptoms. Many consider the therapeutic alliance as the most important "active ingredient" in any therapy. So it is quite important, even for manual-guided therapy. Helpful strategies for engaging adolescents are highlighted in this manual and include the following:

- Use inviting and open-ended questions rather than closed-ended or checklist-type questions to spur adolescent clients to share their experiences, views, and concerns. Treat the adolescents as equals and invite them into a collaborative conversation without forcing answers to questions.

- Spend time understanding the adolescents' experiences and underlying explanatory models for their diagnoses or referral issues, and work collaboratively to formulate treatment goals.

- When possible, bridge your views of clinical issues with the clients' views and seek input from your clients on the acceptability of the treatment plan and markers for improvement.

- Present yourself as an ally to enhance the client-empowered environment. Demonstrate compassion, empathy, validation, and nonjudgmental, reflective, and mindful listening in response to the topics raised by the adolescents, and reinforce progressive participation in sessions with specific and encouraging statements. (Note that empathy is a self-referential visceral reaction, whereas compassion is a response involving genuine feelings to relieve suffering.)

- Actively respond to client topics and maintain confidentiality to demonstrate your role as a committed ally and to give adolescents some authority over their treatment. Offer adolescents the opportunity to suggest topics and situations that can be addressed with the strategies presented in this therapy.

- Provide clear rationales for treatment decisions and activities in developmentally appropriate language to demonstrate respect for adolescent clients as active participants in treatment. This helps to establish therapist credibility, which increases the likelihood of adolescent participation in treatment.

Adolescents rarely refer themselves for services, so forming a therapeutic alliance with parents or guardians is usually helpful. Parents are often responsible for facilitating treatment by scheduling appointments, transporting the client, consenting to treatment, providing clinically relevant information about the client's experiences and behavior, and implementing therapeutic assignments that serve to modify the client's environment. In fact, the alliance with caretakers has been found to relate to parent/family participation in therapy, which in turn is related to client improvement (Karver, Handelsman, Fields, & Bickman, 2006). It is important to create an environment of open discussion with parents and other family members during intake sessions. This can be done by utilizing a semistructured format in which family members are welcome to share their experiences and concerns as they come up. It is important to be sensitive to family beliefs and values and to show interest when parents share information during discussions.

In order to engage both the client and the parents simultaneously, it is essential to find ways to bridge the gap between their perspectives. To do so, you can identify points of agreement to encourage discussion, enlist the parents and adolescent as collaborative team members, and help identify mutually acceptable treatment goals and plans. As usual, clear policies about the limits of confidentiality must be discussed with the adolescent and family. Confidentiality is typically maintained for information the adolescent shares in therapy, with the exception of situations involving risk for physical harm, abuse of a minor, or suicidal or homicidal ideation.

Addressing Cultural and Contextual Factors

Every person—and therefore every adolescent—exists within a cultural and social context, often in more than one simultaneously (e.g., ethnic culture, youth culture, urban or suburban culture). Therefore, culture is another important variable in understanding context and treatment needs.

Many effective cross-cultural techniques have been integrated into the treatment approach described throughout this manual. In the first sessions, it is important to elicit the client's understanding of his or her problem and cultural frame of reference through basic open-ended questions (followed by reflective listening): How do you understand why you are here? What do you think can be most helpful for you right now? What are some of your concerns about coming to therapy? What bothers you most right now? How do you see or understand what the problem or need is? Clients may identify other ways they experience PTSD in their lives; for example, they may have specific physical symptoms that are culturally based ways of expressing distress. Less acculturated youth may be more likely to endorse psychosomatic dissociative symptoms. ("I suddenly feel like my head is in the clouds, and I forget.")

It is important for you to understand the culture of the adolescent and help to identify sources of resiliency within his or her community such as spiritual practices, oral traditions, and cultural identity. This brief case example illustrates how reflecting upon an adolescent's explanatory model and construction of the problem can help:

George

George, a seventeen-year-old Spanish-speaking young man from El Salvador, said he did not believe in or want to rely on therapy because he needed to struggle (*luchar* in Spanish) on his own, was not crazy, and felt quite capable of trying to manage without assistance. The therapist asked him open-ended questions about what it means to luchar: What has helped you in this struggle? What has not helped? How important is it for you to succeed in this struggle? What could make it more possible? What would you like to see change? What are the pros for participating in counseling? What are the cons? From there, George identified the kind of changes he would be interested in initiating. This way of engaging him provided an opportunity for the therapist to integrate wording and concepts that he uses (e.g., luchar) into the psychoeducation component and discussion of what they might be able to do together in counseling. George agreed to keep coming to sessions and continued to develop a positive relationship with his therapist over time.

Youth at risk for negative or harmful outcomes need skills, strategies, and social support to resist and navigate the social challenges in their lives that perpetuate those risks. CT shows promise in that regard. The recovery skills, CR exercises, mindfulness practices, and role-playing activities in this manual are all aimed at helping adolescents navigate their current circumstances, in the moment—the only time that a person can learn, grow, and change.

Emmanuel

Emmanuel, a sixteen-year-old Haitian adolescent, shared with his therapist that he likes to write reggae lyrics in which he talks about his life and how he overcame his difficulties. This young man was very hesitant about participating in therapy, but he was delighted to bring in his lyrics and talk about them. The lyrics contained plenty of material about his experiences, cognitions, and ways of understanding his traumatic history that could be explored using the CT model, and could even help him practice mindfulness by bringing his focus to the thoughts and senses he was describing through his lyrics. Emmanuel's music provided a way for the therapist to connect to him so that they could explore his present feelings in sessions, and CR was then utilized to address the thoughts and other feelings that surfaced. The therapist thus engaged Emmanuel respectfully and collaboratively. The opportunity to share his ideas through his music enabled this young man's alliance with his therapist to emerge.

It is most important to be welcoming, creative, and open to adolescents' understanding of themselves and their visions of how things will improve, knowing that they are the experts in their own lives. Listen, coach, and thus build the alliance necessary for any successful therapy. If you find yourself talking more than the adolescent, then it is time to rebuild the alliance—stop, question, listen, reflect, and support.

The motivational interviewing techniques espoused in this manual, along with the collaborative approach aimed at engaging parents and adolescents, promote these alliances. Whenever communication between clinician and client becomes tense or "stuck," we find that returning to an MI style—asking open-ended questions and listening mindfully, avoiding trying to fix or advise—can help. Following are core concepts to consider and use through the course of treatment with adolescents.

Core Concepts Underlying Motivation, Treatment, and Recovery

Ambivalence and readiness for change, concepts important to the MI approach, refer to the adolescent's mixed feelings about change. For example, the adolescent may believe that quitting drugs or alcohol is a good idea, yet at the same time he or she may not want to quit. Motivational frameworks for substance abuse treatment are based on the assumption that ambivalence about change is normal and expected. Even when people see possible benefits to stopping a negative behavior such as substance abuse, they generally feel undecided about making that change because in some way the so-called negative behavior has served a purpose. For example, drugs and alcohol may have helped them feel calmer or avoid negative thoughts. Sometimes adolescents are ambivalent about changing other PTSD-related behaviors such as sexual risk-taking. At times they are ambivalent about coming to therapy and talking about the past trauma. In response to ambivalence, the therapist's task is to help an adolescent acknowledge and discuss these mixed feelings in a way that helps tip the balance in favor of change, and then have the adolescent agree to experiment with alternative coping skills or behaviors that can help promote change.

To engage adolescents, remember and continue to turn to these three central strategies:

- Use reflective and empathic listening.
- Practice embodied presence.
- Ask open-ended questions.

Reflective and Empathic Listening

If communication gets stuck, you can always return to reflective listening. This refers to making statements to adolescents that express understanding of what they are saying. Reflections can be simple restatements of what the adolescent has said, or they can move in a little deeper and reflect the meaning or feeling implied by the words. The following example shows how the therapist can respond to the adolescent with reflection:

Adolescent: *My parents are always on my case about getting high, and they are always watching me. I think they even follow me around sometimes. They are the problem. They are crazy!*

Possible therapist responses:

Simple reflection, saying what the adolescent has said, but in different words:

They bug you about using alcohol or drugs, and they spy on you about it.

or

Reflection of meaning, restating the implied meaning:

As though they're always trying to figure out if and when you're getting high.

or

Reflection of feeling, restating what you perceive to be the feeling conveyed in the statement:

It sounds as if it's annoying to you, for them to get on your case like that.

You can use any of the above types of reflections to convey your understanding and demonstrate a commitment to listening to your client's perspective. This approach also reinforces the practice of being aware of underlying thoughts and feelings in a given situation. Remember that when trying to reflect the adolescent's meaning or the feeling connected with his or her words, there is an element of guessing involved. Try to keep the guess close to what the adolescent has said. If the adolescent disagrees with the guess, do not become defensive or attempt to explain the guess. Instead, say something such as, "Tell me some more so I'll understand it better."

If adolescents feel they are truly being understood and accepted by the therapist, they will be increasingly open to considering behavior change. Try to accurately reflect the adolescent's mixed feelings about quitting alcohol or drugs using double-sided reflections (acknowledging both sides of the individual's ambivalent perspective) to empathize with his or her mixed feelings:

So you're saying that you really enjoy getting high, but you're worried that it might be hurting your health.

or

You're not sure that you want to stop using alcohol or drugs, but, at the same time, you don't want to get into any more trouble with the law.

Embodied Presence

The concept of embodied presence is associated with mindfulness but is quite compatible with motivational and other psychotherapeutic approaches. The therapist has the intention to be present, as best as possible, to the internal, external, and relational fields of awareness (Siegel, 2007). Relational or attitudinal qualities that underscore the therapeutic interaction include the "beginner's mind" (seeing the situation as if it is happening for the first time), patience, curiosity, empathy, respect, kind regard, and lack of judgment. In order to convey these qualities, you need to be present to your internal landscape of emotions, thoughts, and bodily sensations arising moment-to-moment while listening to the client. Externally, you need to pay attention not only to what the adolescent says but also to the nonverbal cues such as tone, pitch, body posture, facial expressions, and gestures. This is vital to explore perceived discrepancies between what is expressed verbally and nonverbally, as illustrated in this example:

[Using her own body as a barometer to explore something more deeply, the therapist feels tightening in the middle of her chest while the adolescent speaks.]

Therapist: *I'm wondering if we could explore this issue a little deeper.*

or

[The therapist explores the incongruence between what the adolescent is saying and his facial expression and body posture.]

Therapist: *I'm noticing that your brow is contracted, your shoulders are up, your posture is a bit slouched, and you are mentioning how happy you are about the project that you were describing. Is it possible that you are elated about the project but that there are also other feelings present? If this is true, what might they be?*

Open-Ended Questions

Asking open-ended questions enhances motivation because it provides adolescents with an opportunity to reflect upon what they think rather than what the therapist thinks. Open-ended questions invite an elaborative response, whereas closed-ended questions can be answered by a one-word or very brief answer. Table 3.1 illustrates the difference between these types of questions.

Table 3.1 Comparison of Open-Ended and Closed-Ended Questions

Open-Ended Questions	Closed-Ended Questions
Tell me about your early experiences with alcohol or drugs.	How old were you when you first tried alcohol or drugs?
How has your family reacted to your coming here to meet with me?	Does your family approve of your coming here?
What has led to your coming to treatment now?	Did someone force you to come to treatment?
What are some of your goals for making things better for yourself?	Do you feel things need to change?

When you ask open-ended questions, you elicit more of the adolescent's thoughts and feelings about his or her alcohol or drug use as well as PTSD-related distress, which in turn is likely to enhance motivation for change and help solidify commitment to engaging in treatment.

Motivational Interviewing

Researchers and practitioners have described five main strategies that are used in the MI approach (W. R. Miller, 1996; C. E. Miller & Johnson, 2001; W. R. Miller & Rose, 2009; W. R. Miller, Yahne, & Tonigan, 2003; Moyers, Martin, Manuel, Hendrickson, & Miller, 2005). The following descriptions are drawn from concepts found in the book *Motivational Interviewing: Helping People Change* (W. R. Miller & Rollnick, 2012) and in the treatment manual *Motivational Enhancement Therapy for Marijuana Use with Adolescents* (Sampl & Kadden, 2001). Here we describe the principles of MI and how we use these strategies with adolescents with dual diagnosis.

Strategy 1: Express Empathy

The treatment approach described in this manual is not based on confrontation and does not espouse lecturing, criticizing, labeling, ordering, moralizing, or distracting. Rather, the therapist's role is a blend of supportive listener, knowledgeable consultant, and coach. Accordingly, it is important to avoid giving the impression that you are trying to convince adolescents of the error of their ways, and instead show that you are listening with respectful curiosity—the same nonjudgmental curiosity that we are asking them to practice. In fact, much of this work is based on *listening rather than telling.* Although there are aspects of the treatment that include providing psychoeducation and other information, the goal is always to assist adolescents in telling their stories, whether about their PTSD symptoms, drug or alcohol use triggers, or common styles of thinking.

Open and compassionate listening and accurate reflection are crucial to facilitating change. If adolescents feel truly understood and accepted by their therapist, they will be increasingly open to viewing the therapist as a valid consultant to their personal change process and examination of their thinking and coping styles.

Strategy 2: Develop Discrepancy

Motivation for change occurs when people perceive a discrepancy between where they are and where they want to be. To employ this strategy, you will help adolescents recognize the discrepancy between the effects of alcohol or drug use on their lives now and how they would like their lives to be. Awareness of this discrepancy may well drive the desire for change.

Here again, you need to convey respect for the adolescent by avoiding negative judgments and reflecting the adolescent's own stated concerns of how alcohol or drugs use is interfering with his or her goal attainment. For example:

You'd like to get a job at that nursing home, but you figure using pot would make you fail the drug test.

Therapists may find that many adolescents who abuse alcohol or drugs express few goals, especially beyond the immediate future. Therefore, it is essential to listen for what is important to the adolescent in the immediate future. For example:

On the one hand you want to keep getting high, but on the other hand you'd like to get your parents off your back.

Even if they are unable to verbalize any specific goals, some adolescents may have a vague belief that their lives might be better if they stopped using alcohol or drugs. In such cases, it is helpful for you to reflect this positive expectation back to the adolescent, as in the following example:

You want something better from your life than you have now. You're thinking that if you stop using weed, your life might start to go better. Is that it?

Notice that in the previous example, the therapist asks whether she has correctly understood the adolescent. This gives the adolescent the chance to correct an inaccurate reflection and, ultimately, may allow the adolescent to feel better understood.

Another common discrepancy among adolescents is between their current and desired view of themselves. To address this discrepancy, the therapist may reflect to the adolescent:

So you're saying that you feel like a loser when you get high so often, and you don't like seeing yourself that way. You'd like to feel good about yourself again. Is that it?

Strategy 3: Avoid Argumentation

The MI style explicitly avoids direct argumentation, which tends to evoke resistance. The therapist does not seek to prove or convince by force of argument. When MI is conducted properly, the adolescent—and not the therapist—voices the arguments for change (W. R. Miller & Rollnick, 2012).

If an adolescent becomes increasingly defensive or hostile, consider the possibility that your previous comments may have played a role in eliciting this reaction. You may have drifted from a motivational to a confrontational approach. In such a case, you will need to resume the MI style. Again, you can go back to open-ended questions, which are meant to assist in clarification. For example, rather than saying, "I don't understand why you are in school if you don't do the work," it is better for you to ask:

Can you tell me some of the reasons you want to keep going to school, or why finishing school is important to you? Tell me about what keeps you coming back to school, even if sometimes you leave for a while.

Another key to avoiding argumentation is to treat ambivalence as normal and explore it openly, using double-sided reflections. Here are some examples:

You enjoy partying, but you think it's messing up your life.

or

Part of you wants to quit using weed, but you're worried that you'll miss how it makes you feel too much.

These double-sided reflections help the adolescent feel understood. This, in turn, decreases the adolescent's defensiveness, and also decreases the likelihood of further argumentation. Arguments may still happen, but you have done your best.

Strategy 4: Roll with Resistance

The MI strategy does not encourage meeting resistance head on, but rather supports rolling with it. When an adolescent voices opposition to change, you may feel tempted to respond with a counterargument. If you do, however, the adolescent is likely to defend and further strengthen the original stated position. You can roll with the resistance by empathetically reflecting the adolescent's hesitancy to change and then pointing out that it will be up to him or her to decide if and when to change. Here's an example:

Adolescent: *I just came here because of the court. I don't think smoking a few joints is a problem.*

Therapist: *You had to come here because of the court. You don't want someone else telling you what a problem it is for you.*

Sometimes being in a program like this helps individuals get more information to decide for themselves whether using drugs or alcohol is a problem for them or not. In the example above, if the therapist had responded with a lecture along the lines of, "Using pot has already gotten you into trouble with the law, so it surely is a problem for you," the adolescent would likely have become more resistant. When adolescents are genuinely assured that the decisions about change are up to them, they often become more willing to look at the issue with an open mind.

Strategy 5: Support Self-Efficacy

This MI strategy refers to helping develop and support adolescents' beliefs that they can change or respond to things in a different way. This is vital because people who believe that they have a serious problem are unlikely to move toward change unless there is hope for success. Even if adolescents acknowledge that alcohol or drugs are a problem, they may be disinclined to quit or limit use without the belief that they can be successful in making that change. They may be concerned that their PTSD symptoms will worsen if they stop using, and indeed, sometimes anxiety or PTSD symptoms do increase between episodes of drug use. Your role is to help adolescents develop or strengthen their sense of self-efficacy—that they can, in fact, stop or reduce their alcohol or drug use and manage their PTSD symptoms so that they can feel better.

In order to support self-efficacy, you may ask adolescents about previous successful experiences they have had and note the following areas:

- Periods of abstinence from or reduced use of alcohol or drugs.
- Accomplishment in gaining control over another problematic habit.
- Attainment of previous goals once they set their minds to them.
- Attempts at addressing their trauma history or confronting situations of past abuse.
- Regular practice of mindfulness.
- Coping strategies that have helped them or that they have enjoyed, such as listening to music.

Some adolescents may not make the connection between these previous accomplishments and the likelihood of success in meeting their goals regarding alcohol or drug use and PTSD. They are likely to benefit from your help in pointing out this relationship. You may say, for example, "So you're telling me that you were able to stop the cutting. That's great. Since you were able to stop that, which many people find a hard habit to break, you may be equally successful in breaking an alcohol or drug habit."

Reinforcing Motivation for Engaging in PTSD Treatment

Adolescents may be hesitant to disclose details about their trauma or may feel that treatment is unnecessary. Some may contend that they won't stop using drugs unless they can first feel less anxious. The same MI skills discussed in previous sections can be helpful with ambivalence about treatment for PTSD, including reflective and supportive listening and open-ended questioning. One approach is to have adolescents rate their motivation for making changes on a scale of 1 to 10. On that same scale, ask them to indicate how confident they are that they can make that change. What would help them feel more motivated? What would make them feel more confident? Using a decisional balance scheme, ask what the pros and cons of entering and not entering treatment are, given how they feel. What do they envision can be better? What might make things better? Discover what ideas the adolescents can propose and which challenge they may be willing to tackle first. Go where the readiness for change is, and work together on that.

Encouraging Abstinence and Responding to Relapse

The elimination of drug and alcohol use is considered ideal for maximizing adolescents' ability to learn about themselves while substance free. The goal of reaching abstinence is an important one, but it is a process based on an adolescent's evolving readiness to change and his or her increasing competence in using recovery skills and healing practices.

The Goal of Abstinence

While maintaining and embodying a nonjudgmental approach regarding adolescents' alcohol or drug use and their current state of readiness for change, you should encourage them to attempt or work toward abstinence. Adolescents generally shift in their motivation or readiness to refrain from alcohol or drug use completely, so you will need to work with their fluctuating degrees of commitment as they move through the process of change. The MI approach can be a useful tool at various stages of readiness for change (W. R. Miller & Rollnick, 2012).

With less motivated adolescents, the primary therapeutic task is to help them recognize possible negative consequences of substance use and identify and work through ambivalence. With highly motivated adolescents, your focus should be on helping them to verbalize, and thus strengthen, their own motivation for change. Here you will utilize exercises in the manual aimed at developing skills for implementing change (e.g., challenging thoughts that trigger drug use, employing mindfulness-based practices, and using recovery strategies).

Clients should refrain from using drugs and alcohol just prior to sessions. Encourage them to come to sessions and practice the skills at home while sober and not under the influence of drugs, reinforcing that this will be the best way to alleviate their PTSD symptoms and develop skills critical to their recovery.

Above all, adolescents should be given the message that the decision is up to them. Here are some ways that this message can be presented:

I know you're not sure about stopping pot completely. Let's spend some time talking about that. There are some good reasons to think about quitting pot completely. You mentioned a number of ways that pot is causing you problems, like the trouble with your parents and not thinking as clearly as you used to. By stopping pot use completely, you'll have the best chance of learning about how your life could be without pot. How does that sound to you?

or

As you think about what you want to do, I want to encourage you to consider stopping all drugs and alcohol, at least for a while. You'd get a chance to see what that's like so that you can decide what you want to do in the long run. It also gives you more of a chance to learn a lot about yourself—like what sort of things might have been keeping you using drugs—and to help with some of your PTSD symptoms. What do you think?

The key to the above interventions is to allow plenty of time to listen to the adolescent's thoughts about the decision, respond with empathy, and avoid argumentation.

Learning from a Slip or Relapse

A slip or a full-blown relapse should be viewed as a learning opportunity, not necessarily as a threat. Examine the events prior to the slip or relapse, and try to identify the triggers and the adolescent's reactions to them. Were there expectations that alcohol or drug use would meet some need? Was the use of the drug or alcohol in response to a traumatic trigger you have identified? Was it a social, peer-related, or culturally related trigger? Are certain behaviors expected by the adolescent's peer group? Also, what events followed the slip that might impact the likelihood of further use? And finally, how can the client use some newly learned skills to identify and respond to the triggers?

Based on the responses to these questions, help the adolescent develop a plan to cope better with those antecedent events when they occur again, as well as with future cravings. How can the client use some skills learned in therapy to think about or address the situation differently? Can any arrangements be made to reduce the likelihood of future use or to make negative consequences less probable? Practicing and role-playing can be done as part of the fifth step in the CR exercises: implementing an action plan. Inquire about the adolescent's willingness to role-play strategies for refusing drugs or alcohol when offered by peers or for other challenging situations. Be empathetic and supportive, and coach the adolescent through the practice and role-plays. The more that you invite the adolescent to actively participate in therapy and practice in the real-world setting, the more likely change will occur.

Relapse and Urine Screening as a Therapeutic Process

If the adolescent is drug tested at your clinic, office, or elsewhere, it may only be necessary for the test to discriminate the presence or absence of drugs (rather than the amount of the drug used). Marijuana may remain detectable at a standard cannabinoid cutoff level of 50 ng/ml for two to three weeks after initiation of abstinence in people who have been using the drug frequently (daily or almost daily). However, once a negative urine test result is achieved, subsequent isolated episodes of use will likely yield positive test results at this cutoff level for only three to four days (Huestis, Mitchell, & Cone, 1996). Hence, to measure continuous abstinence, adolescents may need to participate in a regular random drug testing program. At each session, obtain a verbal report from the adolescent (and sometimes the parent) of substance use since the last visit. Additionally, you can request a urine screening for marijuana, cocaine, opioid prescription drugs, heroin, benzodiazepines, amphetamines, and methamphetamines, and results can be provided during the next clinical visit.

If the results for substance use are negative (i.e., drugs were not present), use these findings as an opportunity to provide positive reinforcement. When applicable, encourage continued involvement in activities that are incompatible with drug use, as well as association with individuals who do not place the adolescent at risk for drug use. Also ask about challenges encountered during this period of abstinence, particularly problems frequently associated with these times, such as emotional distress or cravings for specific drugs and social situations. Find out what strategies or problem-solving steps the adolescent used to cope with these problems or other high-risk situations (e.g., identified the existence of a problem, generated a list of possible solutions, and implemented one of the solutions). Emphasize the importance of continuing to practice problem solving as one method of preventing relapse and to practice mindfulness and CR to identify and respond differently to thought triggers.

Adolescents whose urine test results are positive should be asked to briefly review the circumstances and context of their drug use. This provides an opportunity to identify triggers and enhance coping. Inquire about potential external factors (people, places, things) and internal factors (emotional distress, cravings) associated with recent use. You may also make a brief reflective statement, such as the following, summarizing some aspects of the adolescent's viewpoint:

It sounds as if you're saying that you're not disappointed that your test was positive for alcohol or drugs because, so far, you are not trying to stop using. You have said that even though alcohol or drugs have caused some problems for you at your school, you enjoy getting high and you do not want to stop using at this time. If you decide to try to quit sometime in the future, hopefully you'll have gotten some helpful information from this program about how to do it.

The main point is that you do not have to fight adolescents or try to make them feel badly about positive urine test results.

When an adolescent disagrees with a positive drug screen result, you may explain that there can be a few different reasons for the discrepancy and that it may never be entirely clear which applies in this case. You can also share the following explanations that have applied to other adolescents and may be possible in this case:

- The positive result may simply mean that previously reported use has left physical traces that are showing up on the test. If the adolescent continues to abstain from alcohol or drugs, subsequent drug test results will eventually be negative. (Obviously this explanation is less likely to be plausible when an adolescent reports more than four to six weeks of abstinence.)
- For a number of reasons, the adolescent may not believe that it is safe to be honest about recent use.
- It may be possible that something has gone wrong with the test (but this is an infrequent occurrence).

At times adolescents may express that they have to use substances because otherwise their anxiety, depression, anger, PTSD, or other emotional states get worse. Here, once again, you can be empathetic and supportive but be explicit about eliciting other ways the adolescent may be able to reduce these symptoms. Consider a further analysis of triggers for PTSD symptoms and explore strategies for addressing them, as in the following example:

It seems that when you used last time it was after you saw your uncle. What were you feeling when that happened? What were you thinking then? Is there something you can do in those circumstances to help you not use? Could you use some of the strategies we have practiced?

Again, the aim is to work collaboratively, with compassion and without judgment, and to be mindfully present to new opportunities that emerge for the adolescent in regard to responding to daily triggers (people, places, and things), thoughts, and feelings.

Chapter 4

Mindfulness-Based Cognitive Therapy for Other Co-occurring Adolescent Mental Health Conditions

Most of us have become deaf to our own bodies,
which is why we are out of tune.

—Terri Guillemets

Anyone who works therapeutically with adolescents with a history of trauma and addictions knows that these young people often have other co-occurring mental health conditions and can also experience many psychosocial challenges. Compared to adults, children and adolescents are more likely to engage in traumatic reenactment, in which they incorporate aspects of the trauma into their daily lives. For example, children may reenact trauma in their play, and adolescents may reenact physical abuse in their romantic relationships. In addition, adolescents with PTSD are more likely than younger children or adults to exhibit impulsive and aggressive behaviors and as a result may end up engaged in the juvenile justice system. It has been shown that sexually abused children can experience fear, anxiety, depression, anger and hostility, aggression, sexually inappropriate behavior, self-destructive behavior, feelings of isolation and stigma, poor self-esteem, difficulty trusting others, substance abuse, and sexual maladjustment (Benoit, 1993; Bonn-Miller, Vujanovic, Feldner, Bernstein, & Zvolensky, 2007; Caffo & Belaise, 2003). Young people who have experienced traumas also often have conflicts with peers and family members, a tendency to act out, and problems with school performance (Caffo & Belaise, 2003). In this chapter we discuss how these co-occurring problems can be considered and addressed as part of your treatment approach with adolescents within an MBCT framework. We will consider some of the supporting research and offer case examples to illustrate the benefits of MBCT, but first we will review these common disorders of childhood and adolescence.

Common Co-occurring Disorders

A number of psychiatric disorders are commonly found in children and adolescents, including youth who have been traumatized and those with addictions. These include depressive disorders; bipolar disorder; anxiety disorders; obsessive-compulsive disorder; ADHD; and disruptive, impulse-control, and conduct disorders. Any of these can co-occur, either individually or combined, with PTSD and addictions. What follows is a brief description of these common disorders based on the *Diagnostic and Statistical Manual of Mental Disorders* (5th ed.; *DSM-5*; American Psychiatric Association [APA], 2013), with special reference to how these may present in adolescents.

Depressive Disorders

The primary depressive disorders are major depressive disorder and persistent depressive disorder (dysthymia).

- **Major depressive disorder** is a serious condition characterized by a persistent sad mood, feelings of worthlessness or guilt, and the inability to feel pleasure or happiness. This disorder typically interferes with day-to-day functioning such as eating and sleeping. Individuals with this disorder feel depressed almost every day, though adolescents may not acknowledge being sad. Instead, major depression can appear as "bad moods" or irritability that persists for a long time. Adolescents with major depressive disorder may also act out with risky behaviors or self-medicate with substances.
- **Persistent depressive disorder (dysthymia)** may be diagnosed if sadness or irritability is not as severe but continues for a year or longer. Adolescents with dysthymia often feel "down in the dumps." They can have low self-esteem, feel hopeless, and have problems sleeping and eating. Unlike major depressive disorder, dysthymia does not severely interfere with day-to-day functioning, but the "down mood" is a pervasive part of the adolescent's world.

Bipolar Disorder

There are two types of bipolar disorder: bipolar I and bipolar II. Bipolar I is characterized by at least one manic episode (often manifest in adolescents as extremely pronounced and persistent irritability and explosive temper), and bipolar II is characterized by at least one major depressive episode and at least one hypomanic (shorter duration than manic) episode. Bipolar disorder (previously referred to as manic depression) often develops in the late teen years and early adulthood and may affect as many as 1 to 2 percent of adolescents (Kessler et al., 2005). Bipolar disorder is highly associated with the risk of developing addictions as a result of impulsivity, mood dysregulation, increased risk-taking behavior, and shared biological (i.e., genetic inheritance) and socio-environmental risk factors between bipolar disorder and addictions.

Anxiety Disorders

Anxiety disorders are among the most prevalent mental health conditions in children and adolescents and are especially common in highly stressful environments. There are many types of anxiety disorders, all of which have one shared trait—prolonged, intense apprehension that is out of proportion to the present situation, or is in response to ongoing stress, and affects an individual's daily life, functioning, and happiness. Symptoms of an anxiety disorder can build gradually or come on suddenly and create a sense of doom and foreboding. Adolescents with anxiety problems may not even know what's causing the emotions, worries, and sensations they are experiencing, and they are prone to self-medicating the anxiety disorder—for example, by drinking alcohol to tolerate social situations or smoking cannabis to relax.

The following are specific anxiety disorders that can affect adolescents:

- **Generalized anxiety disorder.** With this common anxiety disorder, adolescents worry excessively about many things such as school, the health or safety of family members, or the future in general. They may always expect the worst to happen. Along with worry and dread, the adolescent may have physical symptoms such as headaches, stomachaches, muscle tension, or fatigue. Their worries might cause them to miss school or avoid social activities. With generalized anxiety, worries can be burdensome, making life feel overwhelming or out of control.

- **Specific phobia.** This is an intense fear of a specific thing or situation that is not inherently dangerous, such as heights, dogs, or flying in an airplane. Phobias cause people to avoid the things they fear.

- **Social anxiety disorder (social phobia).** This anxiety is triggered by social situations or speaking in front of others. Adolescents with this disorder may fear being judged by others in social situations, causing them to experience anxiety and avoidance of those situations.

- **Panic disorder.** This is characterized by episodes of anxiety that can occur for no apparent reason. During a panic attack, an adolescent typically has sudden and intense physical symptoms that can include a pounding heart, shortness of breath, dizziness, numbness, or tingling sensations.

- **Agoraphobia.** This disorder involves intense fear or avoidance of being in certain situations from which escape might be difficult or in which a panic attack could occur. Examples of situations that can cause agoraphobia include being in public transportation, a restaurant, or a shop.

Obsessive-Compulsive Disorder (OCD)

Individuals with OCD experience obsessions (excessively preoccupying thoughts) and/or compulsions (repetitive actions to try to relieve anxiety) that interfere with their daily functioning. In many ways this can resemble an impulse-control disorder because affected individuals have little control over their thoughts or behaviors.

Attention Deficit/Hyperactivity Disorder (ADHD)

ADHD is a common neurodevelopmental disorder that affects about 10 percent of school-age children and is characterized by inattention, impulsivity, hyperactivity, and executive functioning problems. According to the *DSM-5*, boys are about two times more likely than girls to be diagnosed with ADHD (APA, 2013), though it's not yet understood why. Adolescents with ADHD act without thinking, are hyperactive, and have trouble focusing. They may understand what's expected of them but have trouble following through because they can't sit still, pay attention, or focus on details. ADHD is a risk factor for the development of addictions, especially if paired with conduct disorder (see the next section). It is particularly associated with nicotine use, as it appears that youth with ADHD respond differently to nicotine and have a vulnerability to smoking and nicotine addiction. (Ameringer & Leventhal, 2012; Lee, Fuemmeler, McClernon, Ashley-Koch, & Kollins, 2013). Also, impulsivity and school difficulty can lead adolescents with ADHD to associate with substance-using peers.

Disruptive, Impulse-Control, and Conduct Disorders

Among this category of disorders, two are most pertinent to this discussion:

- **Oppositional defiant disorder (ODD).** The hallmark symptom of ODD is pervasive defiance. ODD is defined by the *DSM-5* as "a pattern of angry, irritable mood, argumentative/defiant behavior, or vindictiveness lasting at least six months" (APA, 2013, p. 462). It was previously believed that a child might "graduate" from ODD to conduct disorder (see below) but could not have both at one time. In the *DSM-5*, however, both diagnoses can exist concurrently. By addressing mood regulation and negative cognitions, MBCT-Dual helps adolescents reduce reactivity to situations, including the impulse to be defiant.
- **Conduct disorder (CD).** This childhood behavior disorder is characterized by aggressive and destructive activities that cause disruptions in the child's natural environments such as home, school, place of worship, or neighborhood. The overriding feature of CD is a repetitive and persistent pattern of behavior that violates societal norms and the rights of other people, such as stealing, threatening, or assaulting others. CD often co-occurs with ADHD, although not all youth with ADHD have CD. When both are present, CD is often the driving force behind risky behaviors such as substance abuse. The younger the age of CD onset, the worse the prognosis. Youth with substance abuse problems often are diagnosed with CD because of the addiction-related behaviors they exhibit (e.g., stealing, lying). For that reason, youth with primary diagnoses of PTSD and addictions often end up in juvenile detention and incorrectly categorized as primarily or solely exhibiting CD. In other words, the other trauma- and addiction-related problems are not identified or addressed.

Benefits of Mindfulness

It is reasonable to be concerned about the complexity of issues faced by adolescents who have experienced trauma and are also plagued by psychiatric conditions. These adolescents often face many psychosocial problems at home, at school, and in their community, and at times they encounter legal issues. Even the most seasoned clinician with experience working with adolescents can feel overwhelmed. But there is a great opportunity to help these young people. Impulse control, behavioral reactivity, and mood regulation difficulties are common issues that adolescents experience, especially those with a history of trauma. Although there is not one simple solution to these problems, MBCT-Dual may be a very significant component of a comprehensive plan, for which you will serve as one member of a treatment team.

Stress reduction and self-acceptance often are two of the major benefits of mindfulness, benefits that are particularly important during the drama- and turmoil-filled period of adolescence. Emotional regulation and learning how to quiet one's mind are invaluable skills. Although the research on mindfulness for children and adolescents is just beginning to gain traction, existing research (for instance, Hofmann, Sawyer, Witt, & Oh, 2010) suggests that for youth who suffer from anxiety, depression, ADHD, and behavioral problems, mindfulness can be especially beneficial. It can help with

- developing increased awareness and attention and decreased distractibility;
- learning to step back and observe thoughts and feelings so as not to overly "drive" one's sense of self or one's understanding of life based on a rigid set of thoughts or perceptions;
- learning to have a more flexible mind in order to reappraise situations (see things differently and more expansively) and control impulsive reactions;
- using body awareness and emotional regulation for improved interpersonal, academic, and social functioning; and
- reframing one's perceptions of oneself and situations and being present in the moment to bring about improved mood and diminished anxiety.

Mindfulness meditation has been increasingly incorporated into psychotherapeutic programs due to the large body of evidence demonstrating its benefits for stress-related symptoms, psychiatric disorders, and somatic illness. In the last ten years the research in this area has grown exponentially from approximately twenty studies published annually in the 1980s to 400 annual empirical publications in the last decade. Mindfulness has been found to ameliorate symptoms related to anxiety (Hofmann, Sawyer, Witt, & Oh, 2010; Roemer, Orsillo, & Salters-Pedneault, 2008), ADHD (Jha, Krompinger, & Baime, 2007; Kravariti et al., 2009; Maalouf et al., 2010; Valentine & Sweet, 1999; Van Dam, Sheppard, Forsyth, & Earleywine, 2011), and substance-abuse disorders.

The research has been enlightening in the area of mindfulness for substance-use disorder. In a pilot study with sixteen heroin users in early recovery, Schuman-Olivier and colleagues (2010) found high levels of improvement in the Observe subscale of the Five Facet Mindfulness Questionnaire. The subscale measures how well an individual develops the ability to be self-observing, especially in regard to body awareness. High levels of this awareness mechanism were associated with decreased drug use among those at high-risk for relapse (Schuman-Olivier, Albanese, Carlini, & Shaffer, 2010). Other research has also found important benefits of mindfulness in the awareness of cravings and urges, impulse and anger control, and the ability to ride the wave of discomfort (Vallejo & Amaro, 2009).

Table 4.1 shows some ways in which mindfulness and cognitive therapy can be helpful for specific types of mental health or behavioral problems. It is important to note that there is significant overlap across problems in terms of what approaches and practices are beneficial. As a clinician you can determine which practices may benefit a particular adolescent to build a practice "tool box," which can help the adolescent address a set of problems he or she is trying to overcome. At the center of mindfulness practice is helping adolescents better manage stress and replenish their "self-regulation tank." This also includes helping them to be compassionate regarding their ADHD, depression, or anxiety symptoms and to know when to reframe unhelpful thinking patterns and change maladaptive coping and self-destructive behaviors. All of the mindfulness practices and CT techniques in table 4.1 are discussed in chapter 7, and specific meditation scripts are found in appendix A. (Guided audio of the meditations is also available; visit http://www.newharbinger.com/31335 to download it.)

Table 4.1 Therapeutic Aspects of MBCT-Dual for Different Emotional and Behavioral Problems

Emotional/ Behavioral Problem	**Symptoms/ Concerns**	**Effects of Mindfulness**	**Effects of Cognitive Therapy**	**Examples of MBCT-Dual Practices and Exercises**
Anxiety	Anxious thoughts; worries; inattention; nervous reactivity	Self-awareness and reflection regarding anxious thoughts and worries; ability to bring awareness to and ground oneself in the present moment and the body; stress reduction	Ability to reframe anxious thoughts	Formal: Sitting Meditation with Awareness of Sounds; Seated Body Scan; Walking Meditation; Nine Dots Exercise Informal: emotion-focused mindful coping; problem-focused mindful coping
Depression	Sad mood; poor focus; low energy; negative self-perception; negative thinking	Increased awareness of the transience of thoughts and realization that they are not always true; compassion and kindness to self	Ability to reframe depressive thoughts	Formal: Loving-Kindness Meditation; Eating Meditation; Pleasant Events Calendar Informal: mindfulness of thoughts and feelings; walking down the street awareness exercise; STOP technique
ADHD	Inattention; lack of awareness; impulsivity; executive functioning deficits	Increased focus, awareness, and persistence; decreased impulsivity	Ability to reframe thoughts about incompetence	Formal: Seated Body Scan Interspersed with Mindful Movement Informal: awareness of breath, sounds, and body sensations; awareness of eating, seeing, smelling, and touching; mindful walking; STOP technique
Impulse-control disorders	Impulsivity; reactivity	Decreased reactivity and impulsivity; increased awareness of what is happening	Ability to consider alternative ways to understand or appraise situations	Formal: Riding the Roller Coaster of Emotions Meditation Informal: mindful walking or eating; one-minute body scans; awareness of breath; STOP technique

Addictions	Impulsivity; automatic thoughts and behaviors; cravings	Awareness of the transience of cravings and ability to move through the cravings (ride the wave); awareness of reactions to triggers	Ability to identify and reframe thoughts that lead to substance use; relapse prevention	Formal: Riding the Roller Coaster of Emotions Meditation; "Autobiography in Five Chapters" Informal: body awareness; STOP technique
Trauma	Reactivity; poor focus; dissociative symptoms; numbing; freezing	Awareness of thoughts, feelings, and body sensations that emerge from trauma triggers; reduced emotional reactivity; increased compassion and responsiveness	Ability to recognize and reframe trauma-related thought patterns	Formal: Mindful Standing Stretching Practice; Loving-Kindness Meditation Informal: awareness of sounds; body scan with eyes open and interspersed with movement; mindfulness of thoughts and feelings

Brown, Ryan, and Creswell (2007) identified five underlying processes of mindfulness that help to illustrate its benefits across mental health and behavioral problems:

1. **Insight** refers in part to the ability to see underneath the superficial aspects of a situation, discern its meaning, and learn from experience. A concept associated with insight is the ability to use reappraisal. Garland, Gaylord, and Fredrickson (2011) suggest that reappraisal is one way in which emotion is regulated in mindfulness. They describe mindful emotion regulation as "positive reappraisal," or the adaptive process through which stressful events are reconstrued as beneficial, meaningful, or benign (e.g., thinking that one will learn something from a difficult situation). A self-report study showed that mindfulness practice leads to increases in positive reappraisal and that these increases mediate a reduction in stress levels (Garland, Gaylord, & Fredrickson, 2011).

   Example: After some period of mindfulness practice, an adolescent begins to see clearly how she has benefited from at least a few relationships in her life. She begins to reappraise her life as actually having provided opportunities to learn how to define what it means to have real and meaningful relationships.

2. **Exposure** (not to be confused with exposure therapy) means being able to be with what is arising, whether pleasant or unpleasant, develop a skillful attitude to relate to experience, and live with discomfort and the unknown. Exposure is a well-known concept in trauma therapy research. In the case of MBCT it relates to sitting with and being mindful of what one is experiencing, exploring what is arising and how it arises, and opening up and responding to the opportunity for healing by using that awareness.

   Example: An adolescent boy begins to notice more clearly how his desire to drink alcohol arises; he recognizes his deep sense of sadness, which is then followed by a strong feeling of anticipation and desire for alcohol. Being aware of these feelings, he begins to explore with curiosity how they are related to sad thoughts and destructive drinking. He begins to respond differently, moving away from impulsively acting and toward abstaining.

3. **Nonattachment** refers to having the intention to be open to outcome. When we are mindful, we are open to what is happening, and to what might result from these events even though it may not be what we expect or desire.

Example: An adolescent girl is willing to have a mindful dialogue with her mother about the domestic violence they both experienced in the past and be open to the outcome. She intentionally prepares herself for the possibilities of what could emerge from that conversation, and she finds that she can be less attached to a preconceived need (e.g., having her mom react in a particular way or give her a particular explanation) in that dialogue.

4. **Enhanced mind-body functioning** refers to the positive impact of mindfulness on physical and psychological health. With mindfulness, we are better able to regulate our emotional responses and to breathe, sleep, eat, and focus well.

   Example: After several weeks of mindfulness practice, an adolescent boy is paying closer attention to his eating and is sleeping better. He is also more focused in school and less impulsive.

5. **Integrated functioning** is at the core of mindfulness and refers to individuals' increased self-awareness and ability to make choices, which in turn allows for new opportunities and a transformation of behavior.

   Example: After building her capacity to be aware of what is happening in the moment through awareness of her body, thoughts, and senses, a young woman learns to respond to potentially abusive situations with more self-care.

At first it may seem impossible for adolescents with multiple and complicated problems to progress in these ways. Change, of course, happens over time, with practice and guidance. Every person has the potential and capacity for transformative change. Feasibility trials, controlled clinical trials, neuroscientific research, and qualitative studies have substantiated the benefits of mindfulness. Findings support enhanced body awareness (Salmon, Lush, Jablonski, & Sephton, 2009), emotional regulation (including reappraisal and exposure; see Neff & Megehee, 2010), self-regulation (Baer, 2003; Carver & Scheier, 2011; Grossman, Niemann, Schmidt, & Walach, 2004), cognitive functioning (Jha et al., 2007; Pagnoni & Cekic, 2007), and attention regulation (Baer, 2003; Brown & Ryan, 2003; Lutz, Slagter, Dunne, & Davidson, 2008; Shapiro, Carlson, Astin, & Freedman, 2006). Research also demonstrates the physiological mechanisms involved in mindfulness, which we address in the discussion that follows as a further foundation for understanding the practice of mindfulness as a therapeutic tool.

Mindfulness and ADHD

At the heart of mindfulness practice is the cultivation of intentionally paying attention to what is happening internally and externally. This is distinctly important for individuals with ADHD. Mindfulness meditation practices (including those found in this book) develop the "muscle" of attention and foster a quality of attending that is infused with a sense of exploration, kindness, and self-acceptance. This is why we guide the adolescent with words such as "when your mind wanders, pay attention to where it went, and gently and firmly bring it back to the object of observation." It is also the reason that while other forms of meditation incorporate practices such as mantras and visualizations, in mindfulness meditation we use the breath, sounds, bodily sensations, thoughts, and emotions. All of these practices build our intentionality of paying attention to what is happening in the moment.

We are all familiar with the myriad of distractions that arise when practicing meditation. Plans, dreams, memories, thoughts of anticipation, and emotions pull our focus away from the object of attention. The cultivation of mindfulness practice helps the mind to gather, quiet, and develop the ability to focus and concentrate with more ease, not only while meditating but also in everyday life. Executive attention or conflict monitoring, that is, being able to keep one's attention on the task at hand while disregarding other stimuli, has been found to improve with the practice of mindfulness. Attention regulation, particularly limited in those with ADHD, is developed early in mindfulness practice, usually after a few weeks of practice.

The following clinical case vignette of an adolescent with trauma, addictions, and ADHD depicts how mindfulness and cognitive therapy practices and strategies can be used.

Ben

Ben is a fifteen-year-old boy who was diagnosed with ADHD at the age of seven and also has a reading disability. Until he was nine years old, Ben witnessed his father, who is an alcoholic, physically assaulting his mother. At that time his father went to jail for other criminal activity and has not been with the family since. Ben reports that on a few occasions he was also physically abused by his father.

Ben's mother reports that Ben was always a hyperactive and irritable child. Teachers consistently described him as impulsive and distractible, and he required an individualized educational plan to help him with his learning problems. In third grade he started taking stimulant medication for ADHD, which was helpful; but once he entered ninth grade, he refused to take the medication. He has been struggling academically and acknowledges that he is impulsive and disorganized, but he feels he can handle it and aims to graduate from high school and attend college. He also admits to being a moody person: he gets angry easily, he is quick to explode, and he has mixed feelings about his father, sometimes feeling anger toward him and at other times wishing he could have him back in his life.

Ben admits that he started smoking cannabis, when he was ten years old. He says, "Weed helps me calm down and to focus, if I smoke I can actually do my work." However, his grades have been poor in high school. In ninth grade he also started drinking beer and rum. That same year he engaged in a physical fight with a peer while they were both drunk, and the peer ended up being hospitalized for head injuries. Ben was arrested and spent two months in juvenile detention for this assault and also for an incident of driving a stolen car. He is on probation and is motivated to avoid drinking alcohol, but he says that he still smokes "two to three joints every day, so that I can chill out." He is not currently taking any prescribed medications. His probation officer referred him for therapy with the goal of addressing his addictions and behaviors.

Consider possible questions and considerations you would explore in working with Ben:

1. What are some of the ways that both ADHD and PTSD are potentially affecting Ben's functioning and behaviors? How does he react to his environment, to others, and to his own thoughts?

2. What change is he motivated to consider and engage in?

3. What does he feel will be helpful for him at this point?

4. What are the pros and cons, in his mind, of smoking weed?

5. How does he think and feel about his drinking alcohol?

6. What are his thoughts and beliefs about his trauma, his father, his family, and himself?

7. What mindfulness practices can we employ to help him to develop his capacity for attention and presence in the moment, and to work with his emotional regulation, reactions, thoughts, impulses, and cravings?

8. What is his level of need for reducing impulsivity, cravings, and anger (inner reactivity)?
9. What other treatment options may be needed along with MBCT-Dual (e.g., psychopharmacology or family-based work)?

Answers to these questions provide a foundation for the development of a treatment plan and therapy goals.

In the course of therapy, Ben continues to feel motivated to refrain from drinking alcohol because he knows the probation officer will be on his back if he drinks, and he never wants to go to detention again. However, he says that he really likes weed, and when he has tried to stop smoking in the past he has just become more depressed and irritable. He is willing to try mindfulness to help him focus and deal with his anger and also to be more aware of his actions.

Over a period of twelve weeks, the therapist works with Ben on his motivation. Together they create a plan based on Ben's desire to maintain sobriety from alcohol, and they consider how he understands weed to be helpful and how it may not be. Ben agrees to practice mindfulness when he has not used cannabis, or at least before smoking, so that he can practice with a clear mind. The therapist and Ben use the body scan to first develop his body awareness—that is, his ability to focus on what he is experiencing in his body when angry or distracted—and then to explore how he might build awareness of what is going on in the moment so as to respond differently. After doing the body scan together in session and on his own over some weeks, Ben has the following dialogue with his therapist:

Therapist: *Ben, after doing the practice* [body scan] *today, what did you feel or think?*

Ben: *I noticed that my back feels really tight.*

Therapist: *What do you think that is? Where is that coming from?*

Ben: *Well, I noticed the other day that I tighten my muscles when I get mad. I had not noticed that before. I really tighten up, like I am trying to keep myself in a hold, like I want to stop myself from punching someone in the face.*

Therapist: *You noticed that the other day?*

Ben: *Yes, I just felt like punching my teacher in the face; he was aggravating me. He just kept saying,* Pay attention, Ben, *and he was explaining something I did not understand.*

Therapist: *So what else did you notice?*

Ben: *I wanted to punch him, and I felt angry, and I started to think about all the other things that bother me lately. I just wanted to march out of the classroom. I just wanted to go home and smoke, maybe call my girlfriend. I just wanted out of there.*

Therapist: *Okay, and how did you respond to all that?*

Ben: *Well, when I started going off to another space in my head, I started to focus on my body; I just stopped and did not react. Then I noticed that I was real hyper. I just focused on my muscles. I did notice what happened. At least, I did not punch him.*

Therapist: *And you did not go right out to smoke.*

Ben: *Yeah, I guess.*

Therapist: *Tell me more about what you were thinking then, if you noticed.*

Ben: *When I was sitting there, I noticed that I felt so tight, but also I was thinking about how I am a chump, how I am never going to amount to anything. Then I was just sad. I like being angry better.*

Therapist: *It is harder to be sad, easier to be angry.*

Ben: *Hell yeah. But at the same time I am tired of being angry...tired of being stupid.*

Therapist: *Well, sounds like you have been having some thoughts that upset you... but you're noticing them... As we were talking about previously, that is the first step in reframing things, seeing things from a slightly different viewpoint.*

Ben: *Well, I don't see the point. Nothing changes.*

Therapist: *But you actually have learned to notice what is happening inside of you and in your body; you actually have a chance at responding differently. You did not punch your teacher. You did keep yourself calm. You noticed what was happening.*

Ben: *Yes, I guess so. Hmmm.*

Therapist: *Can we look a little closer at some of the thoughts, see if we can work with them?*

Ben: *Yeah, okay.*

Ben and his therapist continued to work in sessions, building his body awareness, mindfulness, reframing, and recovery skills and also implementing strategies for applying this improved awareness to help with attention. Ben began to notice when his mind was wandering. He became better at bringing his attention to the moment and focusing when someone was talking to him or when he was engaging in a task. To do this he practiced mindful eating, mindful walking, and body awareness regularly, and over time he began to notice that he was responding to situations more mindfully and intentionally.

Ben: *I noticed that I start moving all around and then I'm lost in class; I start thinking about weed, I start thinking about my girlfriend, basketball, whatever else other than what is happening in class. Then my mind comes back to the class and I am just lost, then I am frustrated, and then I don't even care.*

Some weeks further into the therapy and after regularly practicing mindfulness, Ben acknowledged some improvement:

Ben: *I notice my mind wandering, and sometimes I can bring it back to what is happening. I tell myself, Hey man, what are you doing? Come back. It lasts for a little while. It is a little hard, but it is better than before. You know* (brief laugh), *maybe I am not so stupid.*

Ben progressed in reducing his smoking, although he continues to work on his motivation for completely abstaining from cannabis. He has considered seeking psychopharmacological treatment for ADHD to further improve his academics and to reach his goals, but his attention and impulse control are better.

Mindfulness, Depression, and Anxiety

We operate under the common assumption that things that make us angry, anxious, depressed, frightened, and so on lie outside ourselves—that external factors, situations, or people are the cause. When we begin to pay attention to our internal landscape, we realize that our happiness and our suffering stem from how we relate to what is happening. In mindfulness, the belief is that there is always more right with us than wrong, and that happiness is always present within us—all we need is to connect with it.

Depression, anxiety, and other disturbing emotions prevent us from connecting with the happiness that is our birthright and from connecting with ourselves and those around us. In order to work mindfully with feelings of depression or anxiety, we must allow ourselves to feel, as clearly as possible, with curiosity and compassion instead of judgment, how depression or anxiety is experienced in our body. We can pay attention to the sensations that are elicited when we are feeling depressed or anxious. We can ask ourselves these questions: What is the signature of depression or anxiety in my body? Where do I feel this emotion? What is its texture, color, or shape? How are the physical sensations I feel connected to my emotion? We can become curious about the narratives in our minds and the thoughts that are present without trying to push them away, suppress them, or conquer them. If we get stuck or overwhelmed, we can shift our attention to awareness of sounds, awareness of breath, or any other distraction, with the recognition that we are intentionally distracting ourselves because at that moment we do not have the resources to do that work. (To learn how to work mindfully with emotions, see the Riding the Roller Coaster of Emotions meditation in appendix A.)

What follows are two case examples of the use of MBCT-Dual with individuals whose PTSD and addictions are compounded by depressive states and anxiety.

Paulina

Paulina is seventeen years old and lives in an apartment with her twenty-one-year-old sister. When she was fifteen years old, Paulina's parents threw her out of the house when they found out that she identified as lesbian. She spent two years in foster care, where she experienced repeated physical and sexual abuse. Paulina started drinking alcohol and using painkillers when she was sixteen years old, but she is now motivated to stay sober. She has not used pills in six months, and she has significantly reduced her drinking.

Paulina is able to share that she has been depressed for a very long time. Understandably, she feels abandoned and guilty and at other times angry. At age sixteen she dropped out of school for a while because she was just too tired and unmotivated to go. When describing that time she said, "I was in the pits, and I could not get out." She went to detox for her pill addiction and started working toward maintaining sobriety. She still receives support from the state foster care system but resides with her older sister, with whom she has a fairly good relationship. Paulina returned to school, attending one that offered an alternative path to college. There she reached out to a therapist at the school health center who was able to offer MBCT. At the start of therapy she was still moderately depressed, struggling with her feelings about her family and her past and trying her best not to relapse.

Early in their work together, the therapist discovered that Paulina often felt numb and shut down in situations that reminded her of her trauma and life problems. She often felt sad and alone. She sometimes would sleepwalk and eat in the middle of the night. Paulina often said, "I don't know why this dark mood just comes over me; it just happens."

The therapist first started helping Paulina connect with her body. They practiced mindfulness of sounds first, as Paulina said it made her anxious to focus on her breath, but slowly she was able to progress to mindful breathing. When asked about what she experienced in her body and what thoughts she had after they had practiced meditating, Paulina responded, "It was sort of weird. At first I felt, like, numb. I did not feel anything. But then I started to feel a pain in my stomach. I came back to the breath and that helped me feel less anxious, but I just kept feeling my stomach. And I have no idea what I was thinking."

In the next few weeks, she continued to practice mindfulness meditation. At one point, when asked to focus with gentle curiosity on what was going on with that pain in her stomach, she was able to say, "I feel anger in there, sadness, disgust and disappointment at my family, but also with me. Why did all of this have to happen? Why could they not accept me, love me? Why is this all happening to me?"

With the support of her therapist, Paulina learned to be aware of those feelings and thoughts with compassion. Paulina admitted that when she felt these "bad feelings," she would have the urge to use pills just so she could numb herself. With her therapist, she worked on relapse prevention skills and also practiced "riding the urges"—noticing the way that the urge and desire came in waves, how the waves were accompanied by the sadness, and how she could sit with those feelings and ride them out, and they too would pass. She could accept the pleasant and unpleasant and experience them without being drowned.

One day in therapy Paulina came in crying and said, "I think I don't like myself. Why am I so broken?" Her therapist helped her explore these thoughts, guiding her through reappraisal of where they were coming from and how else she could understand them. Paulina told her therapist that she thought if she was not lesbian, she would have been more lovable to her parents, and perhaps it is her brokenness that keeps making her the recipient of abuse. But at the same time she could not reconcile with her parents, as they had caused her so much harm. The therapist explored this and also guided Paulina in reframing and reappraising how else she could look at it all.

After some sessions, Paulina became more and more aware of her feelings, her body, and her thoughts and was more comfortable with exploring these. She felt ready to do the Loving-Kindness Meditation, in which she wished herself wholeness, acceptance, and strength. She also wished health and healing for her parents. When asked about her experience of the meditation Paulina said, "I can't completely forgive my parents, but I can't keep hating them either. I just end up hating myself. I can't do that anymore."

Paulina kept up with her sessions and her mindfulness practice, and she reported improvements in her mood. She sought out a support system of friends (other queer-identifying youth) and reported to her therapist, "I have found my own chosen family, and I keep working on finding me."

Alexis

Alexis is a fifteen-year-old boy who worries a lot about many things. His mother is a four-year survivor of breast cancer, but he still worries that she may die. In fact, he worries that his whole family may die. His neighborhood does have a lot of violence, so he worries about safety. He also worries that he may not pass tests at school. When he was eight years old, he struggled with separation anxiety, and in third grade he had numerous absences from school as he did not want to leave his mom. Sometimes he still has difficulty going to school, but he has been attending fairly regularly. Alexis admits to worrying and feeling nervous a lot. He has drunk alcohol about five times, and he smokes cannabis regularly in order to feel relaxed.

His therapist introduced him to the Nine Dots Exercise, and Alexis became frustrated trying to solve the puzzle, saying, "I am stupid I guess. I tried to solve the problem for a while, but in the end I just gave up."

His therapist tried to show him that there was a way to look beyond the obvious—outside of the box, so to speak—and in the end he might find new ways to see. Alexis found that interesting but was still frustrated. However, he commented that maybe he could try to "think out of the box." He continued to be very anxious and worry excessively, even in school.

His therapist introduced the Sitting Meditation with Awareness of Sounds as a way to help Alexis practice being more present in the moment. He was initially reluctant but eventually practiced, and after a while he reported to his therapist, "I did that sound mindful thing the other day, and it was kind of good. I was getting really worried about things, and I tried just being mindful to the sounds around me for a few minutes, and I felt like I could be right where I was, and less in my mind worrying about the future. Thoughts kept coming in my head, but I just tried to be there, present in the room, and then I let myself notice what I was thinking, too. I was kind of just noticing it all."

Alexis's therapist continued to guide him in other mindfulness practices, including the body scan, to help him be more aware of his body and senses. They also did the Walking Meditation, which Alexis practiced at home and sometimes even briefly at school. After a few weeks he began to be more and more aware of his body, his thoughts, and how he was reacting to his mind and to situations. "I get really tense, and I freak out a lot, but I notice it more and in a strange way my noticing it more is helping me deal with it. Maybe because you keep telling me to just be okay with it, just notice, it's all right. I kind of notice I am scared that my mom might die, that I might die. But I can see that right now I am okay."

The therapist also worked with Alexis on problem-focused mindful coping. Now that he could be more fully aware of his body, his thoughts, and his reactions to problems, he started to practice new ways to respond to situations, saying, "When I start to worry and become anxious, I can choose to smoke weed, but that's not helping so much; I am trying to figure out how to talk to my mom, how to spend time with her in a good way, enjoying things with her."

What these examples illustrate is that one common characteristic of PTSD, ADHD, depression, anxiety, and other stress-related problems is the individual's inability to connect or inhabit the body and to experience subtle bodily sensations and reactivity. Mindfulness practitioners often report that the practice of attending to body sensations, by practicing the body scan and mindful movement, results in an increased awareness of the body. If this can be done without judgment, then it can lead to an enhanced ability to be in one's own skin with more acceptance, and to sense how thoughts, emotions, and behaviors affect the internal landscape. It leads to more awareness and clarity of external events and more empathy toward self and others.

It has been suggested that being able to perceive the "internal weather," or the awareness of our own experience, is an important variable for empathetic responses. We first need to know how we feel inside before we're able to understand others (Decety & Jackson, 2004). The enhancement of body awareness seems to have relevance for affect regulation and empathic processes. Neuroscientific research also shows that the insula and temporo-parietal junction (parts of the brain associated with neural effects of using reappraisal to both increase and decrease socially driven emotion) are impacted by awareness of one's own body sensations as well as social cognition and empathic responses (Singer et al., 2004). Enhanced functioning of these structures following mindfulness training might also correspond to improved empathic responses and compassion attributed to meditation training (Shapiro, 1982). Supporting this assumption, Tibetan monks with over 10,000 hours of meditation experience showed greater activation of both regions during compassion meditation, a meditation that aims at cultivating feelings of empathy toward the suffering of all beings and the wish to alleviate their suffering (Lutz et al., 2008).

The gradual familiarity and intimacy with bodily sensations, emotions, and thoughts cultivated in all mindfulness practices increases the perception of safety, which is vital for internal and external connectivity, good communication, and a responsive approach, as well as for ameliorating the traditional fight-or-flight and stress-induced "freeze" reactions. By practicing an aware and affectionate curiosity, the adolescent can learn to attend safely to the visceral experiences (via body scan, yoga, and other everyday mindful activities) and have physical and psychological choice, leading to freedom.

Through your guidance, adolescents can learn the practice of mindfulness and find a path to a new awareness and experience of themselves, others, and their lives. In the next chapter we discuss the practice of mindful communication and interpersonal dialogue, which will lead you in further considering the importance of your practice of mindfulness in your interactions with adolescents and your building of a safe and transformative space.

Chapter 5

Mindful Communication

The greatest compliment that was ever paid to me was when someone asked me what I thought, and attended to my answer.

—Henry David Thoreau

It is not enough to learn to be mindful of our internal experience while sitting silently in meditation. It is equally important that we learn to be aware of our inner experience while we are in communication with others. Mindful communication, rather than a method or technique, is a way of being and relating—first with ourselves and then with others. Mindful listening can be deeply healing and transformative. More than simply hearing the words that are being said and trying to understand the content, it allows us to tune in and fully appreciate where the other is coming from, to understand the meaning behind the words, and to recognize how the words are impacting us internally. This chapter offers insights into using mindful communication in your practice with adolescents and introducing these practices to adolescents for their use in sessions and with others.

Mindfully listening and communicating with adolescents is important. If they do not feel heard by their parents, teachers, and others, if their concerns are not honored at home or at school, then behavioral problems, substandard performance, and lack of self-esteem often ensue. However, when adolescents are given the opportunity to express their views without the threat of consequences or judgment, when there is a true seeing of who they are, then honesty and healing become possible. In some ways, we approached this idea of listening in chapter 3, which focused on engaging and motivating adolescents. In this chapter, we aim to move more deeply into the role of mindfulness in your approach and practice in working with adolescent clients.

Equally important, adolescents are well served by learning how to practice mindful communication with their therapist and then with others in their lives.

Many conflicts and problems that adolescents experience on a daily basis are related to their interactions with their peers, parents, and teachers. When you help adolescents cultivate the skill of looking closely at their internal landscape, you are inviting them to establish different ways of interacting with others. The invitation is for them to become more aware of the changing nature of their internal landscape while alone and in the company of others, while attending to what the other person is saying.

Effective interpersonal mindfulness (i.e., mindful communication between two individuals) can be practiced with clients only if you have established a strong intrapersonal (inner and personal) foundational practice. This constitutes the basis of being able to attend to clients in a fully present, compassionate, client-centered way. The intention is that the practice of interpersonal mindfulness in sessions will

1. become integrated into your continued interactions with your clients;
2. promote self-care and prevent burnout from working with challenging situations presented by adolescents; and
3. enable you to teach your clients how to communicate mindfully and skillfully, first paying attention to their own internal terrain, and then being mindful with others.

Interpersonal Mindfulness for Clinicians

Mindful communication, or interpersonal mindfulness, begins with you. This means paying attention, on purpose, with the intention to be present to what the client is saying, moment-to-moment, with affectionate curiosity and nonjudgmental awareness. It also means attending to the impact of the client's words on your internal landscape of bodily sensations, emotions, and thoughts. Finally, interpersonal mindfulness involves practicing mindful listening as well as expressing oneself mindfully. There are a few basic steps to the practice, which are deceptively simple to describe: (1) taking a pause to bring oneself to the present moment; (2) softening or relaxing the body; (3) opening oneself to what is in the moment, as it is, during the interaction; (4) trusting that what needs to emerge will; (5) listening deeply; and (6) speaking the truth with compassion and without blame.

Often therapists and clients fail to understand each other. The same way that the bedside manner of a doctor significantly affects the compliance and trust of the client, the various barriers to communication—lack of genuine curiosity about where the client is coming from; unrealistic or incongruent expectations; and failure to approach the whole person, not only the pathology exhibited—can significantly impact the effectiveness of therapy. Often clients do not fully understand the clinician's explanation of what is needed and are unable to follow the advice given.

As a therapist you have been trained to listen, and most mental health professionals feel that they excel in their listening skills. However, if you begin to carefully pay attention—with kindness and open-mindedness, with the desire to see rather than to judge—you will probably find that you are easily distracted by your loud internal chattering, that you listen selectively, and that you tend to interpret rapidly and make assumptions quickly, without taking the time to verify them. You may often find yourself "lecturing" clients and their family members, asking unnecessary or repetitive questions, and judging your clients when they do not do their homework as you prescribed it. In your eagerness to help them, you might feel frustrated and unsatisfied, and, if these feelings are not attended to and explored, you could eventually come close to or reach burnout.

When we listen to others mindfully, it is possible to observe with clarity and compassion not only our own narrative and habitual patterns but also those of others, and the possibility of finding gateways for shifts in these patterns arises. Most of our pain tends to result from our interactions with others, or more specifically from our loud internal chattering about what others are doing or saying. By instead attending deeply to what is actually being said and to the internal effects of what we hear, we can check to see whether our assumptions are correct and create a healing and refreshing synergy for both our clients and ourselves.

Foundational Principles for the Practice of Interpersonal Mindfulness

There are two overarching, foundational principles of interpersonal mindfulness. The first is being an unbiased witness of what you are hearing from the client. If while listening you find your mind moving into judging, planning, anticipating, or remembering, briefly notice where your mind went and gently and firmly bring it back to the client and what he or she is saying. This action of bringing the mind back is performed thousands of times a day if necessary, without self-criticism and with a lot of patience and kindness for yourself. We can break down this first principle into some key practice components.

What interpersonal mindfulness is:

- Listening to every word of your client as if you were listening to him or her for the first time, infusing a sense of wonder and curiosity. This is sometimes called beginner's mind.

- Trusting in the process, in the innate internal resources of your client to heal, and in your capacity to guide the process with skillfulness.
- Being open to the outcome, to whatever will arise, and to infinite possibility.
- Letting be or accepting what your client is saying or doing, even if it is difficult to hear. Acceptance does not mean resignation, nor does it mean that you cannot be proactive in exploring with the client the internal and external resources available to him or her to work with the situation.

To mindfully listen, it is best to prepare by slowing down before you begin to communicate. Formulate the intention to be present and compassionate. Soften your body and be grounded in it. Remember to inhabit your body while in communication and not to disappear from yourself. Pay attention to the breath for a few moments before you initiate a conversation, especially if the conversation is expected to be unpleasant. Notice if your mind moves into judgment, planning, business, and so on, and escort it back to the words that you are hearing. Listen with intent, compassion, nonjudgmental awareness, and curiosity. There is no need to rehearse what you are going to say next. Be aware of your verbal and nonverbal cues such as tone, pitch, gestures, body posture, distractibility, and timing, as well as whether your spoken words are true or honest, beneficial, and kindly said.

The second foundational principle of mindful listening is approaching our interactions with the intention to serve, which is quite different from an intention to fix. Fixing or helping implies authority and conveys the message that you know more about that person than he or she does. No one, not even the person closest to us, can know more about how we feel in our own skin than we can. When we feel that we know best for someone else, we create dependency. We take away a person's self-efficacy, self-worth, and faith and trust in him- or herself. Put another way, we can listen with our minds or listen with our hearts. The mind's tendency is to compare, judge, blame, help, fix, and criticize. When we listen instead with a compassionate mind and an open heart, we can access our wisdom, innate intelligence, understanding, forgiveness, acceptance, patience, and trust in ourselves and the other. This way of listening has the capacity to heal profoundly, while at the same time enabling the giver—giving from abundance instead of depletion—to avoid burnout and remain fresh and nourished.

We serve with gratitude, for the opportunity to share, and for the happiness that arises when we give to others from the heart. Psychological or chronological time tends to disappear when we serve. We can see and feel the pain because we, too, have been there—perhaps not in the same situation, but we are familiar with the feelings, thoughts, and body sensations that are elicited by difficulties. We understand that we are all "cooking at different degrees of heat" and that we all belong to the community of suffering.

Just as we have learned to live most of our life on automatic pilot (e.g., to drive with enough awareness not to crash, to eat barely tasting what we are eating), we have become skilled at partial, continual listening. This is listening with just enough attention to follow the conversation while the mind is going back and forth into other areas. We are so accustomed to distraction that it has become almost impossible to tune in deeply and to really listen to what our family, coworkers, and clients are saying.

What interpersonal mindfulness is *not*:

The following ways of listening are antithetical to mindful listening and often produce unwanted results.

- Listening like you hear the rain—rather absently, not really interested, but pretending that the interest is there. As a therapist you can leave your body parked on the chair and escape into your fantasies, plans, memories, or "to-do list." You can be aware of what the other person is saying and manage to say whatever is necessary to feign engagement. This might appear relaxing, but it is actually quite exhausting and creates unhappiness in our minds. An article by Matthew A. Killingsworth and Daniel Gilbert (2010), "A Wandering Mind Is an Unhappy Mind," described the findings of their study, which indicated that 46 percent of the time our minds tend not to be present to what we are doing and that the less present we are, the less happy we are.

- Listening with the attitude of "fixing" the other person as if they were inherently broken. This is a common impulse we have as clinicians. We forget that although the client's life appears to be malfunctioning, the client has an innate wisdom and knowledge that is forever present, and your task is to help him or her to access that ever-present wisdom. You may feel that you know what the other person needs, and in a certain way you do because of your training and experience, but you cannot truly and absolutely know what is best, short- and long-term, for that person. You may feel particularly correct in giving advice to young people. But your client will always be the main scientist of his or her own life.

- Listening with a "striving" mind—that is, having an agenda that you want the other person to follow or, if the adolescent makes choices you don't feel are in his or her best interest, listening with criticism and with a judgmental attitude.

- Listening with such intensity and becoming so immersed in what the other person is saying that you lose a sense of yourself and become disembodied. This type of listening can be quite dangerous; what the other person is saying can penetrate so deeply that it is as if that event or circumstance were happening to you. With this type of listening you could experience vicarious or secondary trauma rather easily, as if you are being swept away by the same current that the other person is presenting.

Relating Mindfully with Adolescent Clients: Clinicians' Stories

Trusting in the process is usually the most confusing and difficult aspect of mindful communication initially, but it can be the most useful. These are practices that have been tested thoroughly and carefully crafted.

A therapist working with a very difficult adolescent in a school setting shared the following experience after working assiduously in trusting the process:

> *In our session, the teen had stopped talking to me and was upset because he was not getting his way. I was prepared to begin to recite to him the consequences of his behavior when all of a sudden I paused and became aware of a huge contraction in the pit of my stomach. I realized with sadness that in the last few sessions I had distanced myself and had already given up on this boy. At that moment I remembered the kind counselor who had bent over backwards more than once to help me when I was growing up and how he had persisted until he saw me through the difficulties that had engulfed me for a while. An emotion of gratitude filled me and at that moment I formulated the intention to begin again and to be present for my client, and to do everything that I could do to connect with him. I smiled, and with pain in my heart I asked softly if he was okay. He started sobbing. That moment was the beginning of a truly effective interaction that turned out to be healing for both of us.*

Virginia, a nurse, recently had a visit from a teenage student at her school clinic. She had known her for many years and enjoyed her aliveness and spirit:

> Serena was seen first by an apprentice nurse who was shadowing Virginia for the week. The apprentice reported to Virginia that Serena's presenting condition was better but that she felt she was "depressed" and might have begun to smoke marijuana. Virginia and the apprentice nurse entered the examining room where Serena was sitting with her mother. Virginia asked Serena how she was feeling, and she replied that she was fine. Virginia

asked her about school and whether she had been taking her medication; Serena said that she had, and Virginia encouraged her to continue. After examining her, Virginia left the room with the apprentice nurse so that they could discuss the situation privately. Virginia thought that Serena was fine, but the apprentice nurse disagreed, stating that she had noticed how teary Serena had become at a particular moment during the conversation. When this was brought to her attention, Virginia remembered that quick instance and realized that it had not fully registered because at that moment she was concerned about the many students who were waiting to see her that day.

Virginia returned to the room alone and asked Serena's mother to leave the room. She spoke softly and kindly to Serena and asked if she was really okay. Serena breathed deeply and in a very low and flat voice began to say how she had been betrayed by her boyfriend with her best friend. She expressed that she had been sad for the last couple of months, unable to sleep well, and as a result she had begun to smoke marijuana in order to cope at school. She had promised her parents earlier that she would stop and would never smoke marijuana again. She felt guilty that her parents did not know that she had been smoking again and was afraid that they would soon find out. Virginia and Serena agreed to tell Serena's mom what was happening. Her mother was very supportive. Within a couple of weeks Serena was under treatment for her depression and addiction.

Virginia realized that without the help of the apprentice nurse she would have missed the opportunity to gain Serena's trust and to seek effective treatment for her. That experience allowed Virginia to appreciate the importance of paying attention, as intently as possible, moment-to-moment, during every client's visit.

Hints and Tips for the Clinician

Below is a list of strategies that can help you maintain a mindful approach in communicating with the adolescent:

- Think of your role as exploring the mind and experience of your adolescent client, helping to bring forward his or her thoughts, feelings, and wisdom.
- Listen slowly and deeply: encourage your client to tell his or her story.
- Avoid interruptions.
- Invite elaboration and clarification.

- Consider yourself an explorer whose objective is to learn all you can about your client's stories and what made them possible.
- Take the opportunity to ask questions you are truly curious about.
- Resist the temptation to interpret the story or to agree or disagree.

Additionally, in order to connect with the experience of each session, ask yourself some of the following mindful questions:

- What were you feeling in your body during the interaction?
- What did your breathing feel like?
- Was there tension in your body? If so, where?
- What about the experience was pleasant? What about the experience was unpleasant?
- What emotions were you experiencing? When have you felt this way or found yourself in this situation before?
- What kinds of thoughts were you having?
- What aspects of this situation made you feel satisfied? In what way?
- What aspects of this situation made you feel uncomfortable or afraid? In what way?
- What characteristics of this person do you feel drawn to? Why?
- What characteristics of this person make you feel repelled or irritated? Why?

After sessions, when possible, ask these additional questions of yourself:

- What did I notice that was unusual?
- What data might I have ignored?
- What interfered with and what facilitated my ability to be attentive and observant?
- What about this session was surprising or unexpected?
- What am I assuming about this client that might not be true?
- How might my previous experience affect how I am approaching this client?
- How did I manage to avoid premature closure?

- How might taking a fresh look at the situation alter my diagnostic impression?
- Was I really present for the client and family, or somehow distracted or distant?
- How did this encounter affect my relationship with this client?
- Were there any points at which I was particularly present? Or distracted or uninvolved?

The cultivation of the qualities of interpersonal mindfulness requires regular practice, both informal and formal. Informal practice occurs during the moments throughout the day when we open our awareness to be as attentive as we can be to what we are saying and how we are saying it, to our gestures, our tone of voice, our body posture, the emotions that are present, the feeling tone, and its signature in our body. We also pay attention, as intently as possible and with a nonstriving and gentle attitude, to those around us when they are speaking. Formal practice takes place during a time that we negotiate with a colleague, family member, or friend to practice listening to each other, for a set frame of time, without interrupting, and practice mindful communication.

Teaching the Practice of Mindful Communication

Now that you have gleaned how to develop your own practice of mindful communication, we turn to a focus on teaching mindful communication practices to your adolescent clients.

Insight Dialogue

Insight Dialogue is a dyadic practice, disseminated in 2007 by Dr. Gregory Kramer in his seminal book, *Insight Dialogue: The Interpersonal Path to Freedom*, that helps us learn to connect with others in an openhearted, balanced, and peaceful way. The invitation in this practice is very similar to the guidance followed when we are meditating individually. A description of this practice is the invitation to be present, on purpose, moment-to-moment, to the verbal and nonverbal communication within and between us and the other, holding the context lightly in the background of awareness, with an attitude that is nonjudgmental, curious, and compassionate.

This practice is an effective way—and serves as a laboratory—to see clearly our automatic habits and patterns in communication. While being compassionate with ourselves, we can make different choices and adopt new ways that will take us from scripted, aggressive, or passive ways of communicating into fresh and self-nourishing pathways of relating in order to have a life that is awake, supportive of others, and accepting of the support that we need.

As a therapist you can use this practice with your adolescent clients (or in pairs within a group setting), and you can also encourage your clients to use this practice with their parents or others. To make the process easier at the beginning, if you are not there to guide them, the two people who are going to practice can refer to a printed set of steps.

The individuals who form the dyad sit opposite one another, facing each other, approximately at an arm's length apart, checking that the distance is wide enough for each to feel safe. The individuals select who will be the listener and who will speak first. This is a practice of equality and listening to the other person. The clinician or dyad selects a topic to be addressed. It could be related to a recurrent theme addressed during the sessions or an area that will benefit from a deeper exploration such as addictions, health, frustration, parents, or peers.

Both individuals close their eyes for a moment and are gently and softly invited to pay attention to the sensations, emotions, and thoughts that are present. This is followed by a short awareness of breath meditation to bring the mind into the present moment.

The guidelines for the exercise that follows are to (1) not interrupt when the other person is speaking; (2) notice if there are impulses to give advice, to fix, to affirm, to agree, and to choose to respond instead of reacting to the impulse; (3) notice when the mind moves into memories, regrets, plans, or thoughts of anticipation and gently and firmly bring it back to what the other person is saying; (4) apply embodied listening, that is be connected and grounded in the sensations within the body; and (5) not rehearse but trust emergence, that is, trust that whatever needs to be said will arise.

Next, the individuals in the dyad are invited to follow these steps:

Pause: Stop for a few moments to disconnect from other activities of the mind and formulate the intention to be present. The attitude is nonjudgmental, curious, and compassionate.

Relax: Soften the body and do a few shoulder and neck rolls, if helpful.

Open: Expand your energy, observe the inner bodily sensations, and be open and attentive to the verbal and nonverbal components of what the other person is saying.

Trust emergence: Do not try to rehearse or think too hard about what to say. Just allow whatever you need to say to be said. Trust that what is important to be said will be said.

Listen deeply: Understand that we can only listen deeply when the mind is quiet. Do this time after time without criticizing yourself.

Speak the truth—be honest: Don't try to make the other person feel better; just be you, honest and open. Show that you, too, are vulnerable and imperfect like anyone else. In speaking the truth you are not judgmental or attacking but open and truthful.

Instruct the dyad (or the adolescent with whom you are practicing) to stop periodically to notice habitual stories and routine reactions and to formulate the intention to release them, meeting each moment with freshness, curiosity, empathy, and wakefulness. The allotted time for the exercise is usually three minutes per person. Meditation bells, which are commonly used when guiding mindfulness meditations or other practices, can be rung softly three times at the beginning and end of the exercise.

At the onset of these interpersonal mindfulness practices there is usually a profusion of emotions and thoughts. Pausing becomes more and more frequent as time unfolds. The excitement and attachment to what it is being said gradually decreases. As with any other activity, gradually what we practice tends to become second nature. We begin to inject pauses while in communication with peers and others. The dyad cultivates mindful acceptance and compassion while listening and speaking and formulates the intention for these qualities to increase. In the practice of interpersonal mindfulness we begin to observe the universality of emotions and thoughts and come to understand that in reality we are all very similar, that we are all one. We see clearly that there is no one with a perfect life, that just to be in a human body implies having pain, stress, and times of confusion and doubt. At the same time we begin to recognize that we are all heroes—brilliant, creative, and amazing beings.

Mindful Listening Practice

This is a three-part exercise that can be conducted with an adolescent dyad, in a group setting. First, one person speaks and the other listens without interruptions; second, following a pause, the listener reflects back what he or she heard as closely as possible, using the same words (if recalled) that the speaker used; finally, the speaker takes a few moments to correct the listener if what he or she reflected was inaccurate. To break this process down more specifically, proceed through the following steps:

1. Break adolescents into pairs.
2. Ask them to select who will initially be the listener and who will be the speaker, or, if you wish, you can select the person who will speak first.
3. Invite the adolescents to pay attention for a few moments to the movement of the breath in their belly, maybe asking them to place a hand there to feel the expansion and contraction.
4. Mention to the adolescents that it is normal for the mind to get distracted when listening to others. Ask them to formulate the intention to be present as best as they can, and whenever the listener's mind wanders away from the speaker's words into thoughts of anticipation, memories, or the recognition that *that happened to me too*, to bring the attention back to what the speaker is saying at that moment. If this happens many times, encourage them to just bring the attention back to the person every time that it occurs, with patience and a smile.
5. Ask the adolescents to agree not to interrupt each other. If the impulse arises to interrupt, have them practice the STOP technique (discussed in chapter 7) for communication: stop; take a breath; observe the thoughts, feelings, and sensations in the body connected to the impulse of interrupting while choosing to remain silent; and proceed. Every time this is practiced, the "muscle" of choice and freedom gets stronger.
6. Provide a topic for practice so that the first speaker can begin. Practice topics can cover a wide range of subjects and can be introduced as questions: How are you coping with the challenges that are present in your life right now? What is challenging for you at this time? When do you usually feel stress? What makes you happy? When, with whom, and in what activities do you tend to go on automatic pilot? In what activities do you find yourself more mindful? What are risky situations for relapse?
7. After about three minutes, have them stop and switch so the speaker becomes the listener. The same or a different topic can be offered. The first practice can involve listening for content, and the person who is reflecting can begin by saying, "I heard you say..." The second practice can involve listening for the meaning behind the words. The person reflecting can begin by saying, "I feel that what you said was..." This time, the person reflects the emotions or feelings that the speaker was expressing with words, body posture, gestures, tone, and pitch.

Encourage the adolescents to practice mindful interpersonal communication in their daily lives. Remind them that they can teach this to others as well, and that there are times when using the intentional process of mindful communication may turn around an otherwise potentially conflictual situation.

Intentionality and Commitment

Interpersonal mindfulness will not happen spontaneously; it needs to be cultivated, and it requires discipline, commitment, and intentionality. This is the message for you to embrace and relay to the adolescent. A good part of the learning occurs through the experience the adolescent has with you, the clinician, and through your intentionality and commitment to mindful communication.

Earlier in this chapter we discussed the importance of engaging in your own informal and formal practice of mindful communication. It is equally important to encourage and inspire your clients to do the same. You can explain that the formal practices (Insight Dialogue and mindful listening) are like the gasoline in the tank of our automobile, the reservoir that is there to be used. It is the time that we are open to just practice mindful communication with one another. Informal practice can be explained as the daily ongoing communication, those moments when we are communicating that we stop and pause, gather ourselves, observe our posture and the sensations in our body, pay attention to our thoughts, feel the emotions that are present, and come back to pay attention, as well as we can, to what the other person is saying. Informal practice is anything that we do while speaking or listening, knowing or being aware of what we are doing. This is an important message to convey to adolescents to consider as they engage in encounters each day.

Interpersonal mindfulness is experiential; it cannot be learned just with the mind. A message you can offer the adolescent regarding mindfulness and mindful communication is that the power of mindfulness can only be felt if you take the time to practice. Mindfulness is similar to joining a health club in that you can pay a very high fee for having access to sophisticated equipment and trainers, but if you don't show up, you will never achieve your desired result of being fit; likewise, if you do not do the mindfulness practices on a regular basis, you will not experience their full benefits, such as the ability to better cope with stress. At times you may feel like practicing, and at other times you will feel that you do not have the time or that it is too boring or too frustrating. The invitation is to "just do it," even if you don't like it or find it difficult to open the space for it. It is so common to place our health in the hands of experts without taking responsibility for our own part (even if we swear that that is the last thing we want!). It is also hard to take the time to honor each other in our communications, never mind in ourselves.

Practicing Insight Dialogue with another person allows the participants to receive and offer support with an aim to see things as clearly and accurately as possible. It creates a space where respect, balance, and all other dynamics of relating successfully with others can be seen and clearly honed so that both individuals can bring the same qualities into their everyday lives. Eventually each interaction becomes an opportunity, whether pleasant or unpleasant, to observe with clarity and compassion the desire to dominate, to control, to manipulate, and to want others to make decisions that only we can make. The practice of Insight Dialogue or interpersonal mindfulness is portable and accessible, as it is the practice of mindfulness in the midst of daily interactions with others.

And as for you the clinician, mindful communication allows you to tune in and listen reflectively instead of listening with the aim to fix and give advice. It helps you learn to listen without interrupting, allowing clients to finish their sentences and to complete the ideas that they want to convey. It permits you to observe your bodily sensations, emotions, and thoughts, whether they are pleasant, neutral, or unpleasant, and to remain embodied when listening instead of allowing your mind to roam around. It helps you in formulating and acting intentionally rather than being in the automatic mode. It is an important tool to stop the extra narratives and mental construction of stories we all tend to create about what is happening. It keeps the work of therapy fresh. You can then approach therapy with patience and trust in the generosity of the process itself. It helps to keep you humble, knowing that your clients are the scientists of their own lives no matter how confused they may appear on the surface. It helps you to remember the mystery of life, where all possibilities can be explored. Lastly, it moves you to realize that all true and lasting healing comes from inside and that at the center of therapy is the act of pointing to the inner resources available in every person.

Part 2

Conducting MBCT-Dual Sessions

Chapter 6

General Considerations for Conducting MBCT-Dual Sessions

Mindfulness helps us freeze the frame so that we can become aware of our sensations and experiences as they are, without the distorting coloration of socially conditioned responses or habitual reactions.

—Henepola Gunaratana

MBCT-Dual is an integrated therapy approach for helping adolescents recover from addictions and trauma. Within this program, you have the opportunity to incorporate the entire set of core MBCT-Dual skills including mindfulness meditations and practices, cognitive restructuring (CR), recovery skills, Insight Dialogue, role-plays, and other interactive strategies and practices. Structuring each session will help you to cover essential aspects of the therapy and build upon skills, deepen practice, and create a sense of security for your clients. This should not be a rigid structure but rather one that allows you to offer a predictable flow and approach.

Although the program allows you to be flexible and respond to the specific needs of the adolescent, the following important guidelines and suggestions will assist you in organizing and pacing therapy around the central treatment approaches we have presented throughout this book.

Structuring Sessions

Having a predictable structure for each session helps build a sense of trust and safety for your clients. The duration of meetings can be flexible but ideally should be close to an hour. Let the adolescent's attentiveness and engagement guide you. Writing the day's objectives on a flipchart before the session is helpful for both you and the adolescent to keep focused. If you find that your client is becoming lethargic or disinterested, invite him or her to join you in standing up to do some shoulder and neck rolls, stretching the arms above the head while holding one wrist and then the other. There is often a lot to cover in a session. In addition to addressing what is happening in the daily life of your client, you will offer the opportunity for the adolescent to learn and practice new skills that can be helpful within that daily experience. A predictable structure enables the adolescent to count on having time to share important issues that have come up in the past week; time to practice mindfulness; and time to consider how the practices and skills being learned in therapy can be applied to current situations, feelings, and experiences. A recommended overall flow for each session (after the first introductory meeting) is as follows:

1. Start with a guided mindfulness practice, then process the practice (10 minutes).
2. Provide an opportunity for the adolescent to take a brief moment to connect inwardly and to describe in one word what is present in the moment cognitively, emotionally, or physically (2 minutes).
3. Review the content and assigned practice from the previous session as well as intentions and goals for the current session (5 minutes).
4. Assess how things have been for the client in the last week (5–10 minutes).
5. Engage in core skill practice such as CR or mindfulness for stress reduction, using current life situations and experiences if possible (30 minutes).
6. Develop a plan for home practice, assessing the client's motivation (5 minutes).
7. End with loving-kindness phrases or another closure activity (5 minutes).

Introducing the Mindfulness Practices

Unlike other aspects of talk therapy, mindfulness meditation may be a new experience for adolescents, so it is especially important for you, the therapist, to feel comfortable. You will introduce the concept of mindfulness in the first session, and in the second session a guided mindfulness meditation will be practiced for the first time, for approximately ten minutes. Adolescents may feel strange about doing this and may have many questions; just allow them to ask. You can address some of the science behind mindfulness as well as how it has helped others. Invite the adolescent to choose whether to meditate with his or her eyes closed, or open but gazing down, and guide the meditations in a natural voice. As part of your mindfulness practice at the start of each session, consider practicing a few stretches while guiding and doing the meditation along with your client. This will set a tone of equality, partnership, and openheartedness from the very beginning. It will provide self-care for you, the clinican, and will help the adolescent inhabit the body more and be more receptive to what follows.

The brief mindfulness practices will also refresh and nourish you in your role as the therapist so that you might feel less depleted at the end of the day. Scripts for guided mindfulness meditations are found in appendix A. As you become more comfortable with the manual and protocol, you can use your creativity and adapt the activities to match the adolescent and your work together while still offering the key skills and practices that are central to the therapy.

After the mindfulness practice is completed together, take the time to process it with the adolescent. Use open-ended questions regarding what the adolescent noticed or experienced during the practice, including any challenges or difficulties. Exhibit genuine curiosity and inquiry, reflecting back to make sure that you understood correctly. If the adolescent begins to move into an explanation or a story, gently and kindly bring him or her back to the direct experience of body sensations, emotions, or thoughts occurring in the moment through questions:

What do you feel in your body while you speak about this? What feelings or emotions are you sensing right now? Maybe fear, anxiety, frustration, joy, or peacefulness? Maybe you feel happy or sad?

Some adolescents may feel uncomfortable expressing emotions, so naming a few can be helpful to them. They just need a little practice.

If the client mentions feeling nervous, you can inquire about that feeling:

Where in your body do you feel anxiety or nervousness? Sometimes one can feel anxiety as butterflies in the stomach or as a headache.

You might also say,

It is hard to detect how we feel sometimes. If that is happening to you, can you see if there is a general feeling of pleasantness or unpleasantness? Or maybe there is a neutral feeling, nothing particularly pleasant or unpleasant? Take a moment and allow yourself to feel whatever you are feeling right now. If you like, you can give yourself credit for allowing whatever is showing up for you to do so. And if you are not feeling like giving yourself positive feedback, that's okay, just notice that. No need to change anything. Just become aware of what is happening inside you, in your thoughts or in your body.

Proceed with a brief one-word check-in, saying, for example,

If you like, you can close or lower your eyes for a moment. Notice how you are feeling right now and in one word express anything that you can detect right now.

The client might offer a word such as peaceful or anxious, sad or curious, in pain or just bad. Support him or her and give positive feedback for becoming aware of these feelings.

After the one-word check-in, inquire about the adolescent's practice at home. If a client did not find time to practice, try to elicit what he said yes to doing during the time he had intended to practice: maybe going out with friends or watching TV.

Next, introduce the intentions for that session using a flipchart or sheet of paper, which you can prepare before each session. Engage the adolescent in a brief review of new material and begin the exercises and material for that day. Ask open-ended questions about the material to assess comprehension throughout the session, for example,

We have just talked about some potentially helpful strategies. Tell me how you think these may be helpful for you or not.

Note areas of particular difficulty or confusion, and clarify as needed. Ask about the client's motivation:

How important is it to you to make the changes you spoke about or to try your plan? How confident are you that you can do it? Is there anything else that you think might help you feel more confident?

Consider ending the session using loving-kindness phrases such as these:

May I be safe and protected. May I learn to accept myself and accept others as they are. May I be happy, may I be peaceful, may I be well. May all beings be happy, peaceful, and well.

You can use similar sentences that will help that particular client, or, even better, use ones derived together with the client. If seeking approval and pleasing others is an issue for a particular adolescent, consider phrases such as,

May I trust in my own abilities. May I offer approval to myself instead of waiting for another person to approve of me.

It may feel a little uncomfortable to the adolescent at first, but perhaps if you use some of his or her own language and ideas it will seem more natural. One adolescent came up with this succinct yet powerful phrase:

May I learn to give myself a break.

These phrases are offered at the end of sessions to help reinforce loving-kindness to oneself and bolster the intentions expressed in the phases. During one or more sessions, you can dedicate more time to the full guided Loving-Kindness Meditation. You can also close the session with a poem, a quote, or the lyrics of a song and a few mindful breaths to solidify and support the good work done that day. This is where creativity can enter. The important thing is to build a space where mindful awareness can be learned and become a regular and helpful practice.

The Importance of Practice

Practice is important for both clinician and client; therefore, opportunities to practice before, during, and after each session are highlighted for both of you throughout the program. At the beginning of each session you will find boxed text entitled "Clinician Practice," which includes some recommendations to guide your own practice of mindfulness before the session and to enhance your work in the given session. We do this in order to help sustain you in your own practice of mindfulness, as a tool for your own well-being and for the benefit of your adolescent clients. Why? Because if you are more present and mindful in the session, then you are more available to the adolescent and open to the possibilities of what is happening in the session.

Offering opportunities for the adolescent to practice both in and out of session is also very important. You may give adolescents the handouts to complete and/or review on their own if they are able to do so. More importantly, encourage the adolescents to practice the skills at home (e.g., mindfulness, mindful breathing, inventory of feelings and thoughts, pleasant and unpleasant experiences, coping skills for dealing with cravings) without judgment but definitely with encouragement. There is also time allocated for practice of these skills within the sessions.

Make your sessions interactive, engaging, and creative. Use all of your well-developed skills to ensure that these sessions are responsive to the adolescents' needs while sharing new ideas and options for their consideration and new practices for their exploration and benefit. As discussed earlier, it is important for your clients to agree to try to refrain from using drugs and alcohol and not be intoxicated or "high" when coming to sessions and when practicing skills. For these to be most beneficial, both of you must be fully present.

If possible and appropriate, meet with the parents or a supportive adult, guardian, or mentor of the adolescent's choice some time during sessions 8 to 10. Often parents are struggling with shame, guilt, or anger about family trauma, so exposure to the psychoeducational material and relaxation modules can be helpful. Adolescents can help teach their parents or other adults about CR and styles of thinking or recovery skills, and doing so can help reinforce their command of the skills. This parent-child session also provides guidelines for using mindfulness with the family, which was discussed in chapter 5 in the form of Insight Dialogue and mindful listening practice. Present-moment awareness, self-kindness, and self-forgiveness are emphasized to the parents to help them heal and respond mindfully to their child's behaviors and to their own.

Materials for Sessions

Manual: Keep this manual nearby and available to help guide the sessions.

Flipchart and markers: Prior to each session, we recommend that you write down the goals and intentions for the session on a flipchart to review with the adolescent during the session.

Handouts: The *Client Workbook* includes handouts and informational material to support the sessions. Downloadable copies of this resource are available at http://www.newharbinger.com/31335 and can be printed for use by the adolescent. Please see the very back of this book for more details.

Guided meditations: Appendix A includes guided mindfulness meditation scripts. Audio recordings of these guided meditations, available for use by you and by the adolescent at home, can be downloaded at http://www.newharbinger.com/31335. Please see the very back of this book for more details.

Meditation bells: You might want to purchase a set of meditation bells (usually called Tingshas) at http://www.dharmacrafts.com or any other place that sells meditation supplies. They cost between twenty and twenty-five US dollars. You can also use a soft bell sound such as that found on a cell phone. If you decide to use meditation bells, you can explain that there are no religious connotations to the bells; they are simply a way to signal the beginning or end of a practice or exercise in the session.

Folder of poems and quotes: Poetry and quotes are very powerful tools to inspire and illustrate the work at hand. It is helpful to collect poems and quotes to read to a client to support a particular point that you are making or to highlight an area that you are exploring. We invite you to consider reading a poem or a quote in most sessions. Please see appendix D for a list of recommended poems, but also feel free to identify some yourself or invite the adolescent to find and select poems, quotes, or song lyrics to include during the session.

You are now equipped to begin practicing MBCT-Dual.

Chapter 7

MBCT-Dual Therapy Session Guide

Whatever the present moment contains, accept it as if you had chosen it. Always work with it, not against it.

—Eckhart Tolle

The aim of this chapter is to bring together all of the preceding information about this approach and to guide you through each session of this twelve- to sixteen-week therapy program. For each meeting, we provide preliminary information, a meeting outline, and a detailed meeting guide. Within each detailed meeting guide, sample dialogues are in italics, references to handouts are in bold, and mindfulness practices are indicated by the word "Exercise."

Meeting 1: Introduction, Feedback, and Safety

This introductory session focuses on building rapport, sharing with the adolescent the results of any clinical assessments completed, and discussing what these assessments suggest about his or her strengths and needs. Also central to this session are motivational strategies aimed at helping the adolescent engage in therapy and consider the potential gains and risks of doing so. Additionally, this is an opportunity to introduce an awareness of breath practice and the significance of poetry, which is always placed centrally in mindfulness. Some of the poems you might wish to read in the first session are Mary Oliver's "The Journey" or Rumi's "The Guest House" or "Two Kinds of Intelligence" (see appendix D for suggested poems). We also invite you to use meditation bells to begin and end each meditation.

Meeting Preparation

Clinician Practice To prepare for this first session, take three minutes to practice mindful breathing right before you meet with the adolescent.

Materials

- Flipchart and markers*
- Handouts 1–5
- Meditation bells
- Folder of poems and quotes

* Prior to the meeting, you'll write the intentions for the session on the flipchart, based on the meeting outline.

Meeting 1 Outline

A. Welcome and build rapport (5 minutes)

B. Feedback on assessments (10 minutes)

C. About the program (5 minutes)

D. Weighing my options (20 minutes)

E. Safety plan (10 minutes)

F. Mindful breathing (3 minutes)

G. Inspirational reading (3 minutes)

H. Assign daily practice (2 minutes)

I. Closing (5 minutes)

Meeting 1 Detailed Guide

A. Welcome and build rapport

The focus of this first step is to meet and build rapport with the adolescent. Introduce yourself to the client and spend a few minutes engaging in conversation to get to know each other. Briefly explain what can be offered in the therapy.

B. Feedback on assessments

Offer a very brief overview of the outcomes of assessments, as in this example:

When we asked you the written questions about how things are for you right now, it turns out that you scored high on questions about depression [or whatever applies]. *There were also some answers you gave about drinking alcohol a lot and using drugs.*

What do you think about this information? How do you see those things? What do you think could help? What would you like to see change if anything?

I would like to tell you about how we might work together on some of these things.

C. About the program

Below is a sample explanation of a program introduction. It is presented here as a suggested script, but it will be most effective for you to gain a sense of the information and present it in a conversational tone, allowing for dialogue as well as questions asked by the adolescent.

This is a program for teens who have lived through very stressful times in their lives. You may still have a lot of stressful things happening in your life now. You will learn about something called mindfulness. Mindfulness helps us notice more about what we are thinking and feeling. Time after time you will be invited to be kind and patient with yourself. There might be ups and downs in this journey, but one thing is certain: you are the scientist and the expert of your own life. So, we will work on your goals and with situations that you focus on.

The work we do together may help you feel better by helping with upsetting feelings and thoughts that can be linked to stressful events in your life. I will serve as something like a coach and counselor because we will have the opportunity to explore and practice a set of skills and practices that can be helpful with challenging or stressful situations and emotions. The program has worked with other teens who have also gone through some very stressful experiences and also with people who have had some struggles related to drugs and alcohol. It won't be necessary for you to tell over and over again what has happened to you in the past. This is a program more focused on helping you in the moment and dealing with what you have going on in your life now. We will meet about once a week for about three to four months, for a total of about twelve to sixteen sessions. In the end, you will set your goals.

Here you may reference some of the motivations or goals that the adolescent has already brought up. Show **handout 1: About the Program**.

As your therapist, I will be a guide to help you learn and practice new skills or practices that may be helpful for you in achieving those goals or intentions that you have for yourself. I will briefly describe each part of what you will be learning and doing:

> **Psychoeducation:** *We will discuss some important information, including the common reactions to trauma. You will find out more about what post-traumatic stress disorder, or PTSD, is. PTSD symptoms are learned responses to stressful life situations that can be unlearned. The remainder of the program involves teaching you ways to become more aware of these learned reactions and to be able to respond differently. You will learn about recovery from drug and/or alcohol use. The brain has the capacity to renew itself, and the damage that has occurred due to painful or hard experiences can be healed. Memory and concentration can also improve when we pay attention on purpose, moment-to-moment, and without judging ourselves, situations, or those around us.* [Show **handout 2: PTSD, Drugs, Alcohol, and the Brain**.]
>
> **Cognitive restructuring or reframing:** *Cognitive restructuring involves learning to recognize thoughts that make you upset. You will learn ways to increase your awareness of these thoughts. It is also an opportunity for you to learn to identify how thinking in certain ways can lead us to feel sad, anxious, or angry. Then, we will practice a technique for becoming aware of situations that bring up these thoughts, exploring the thoughts with curiosity and seeing if there is another way to think about these situations. We call this "reframing the thought." You can also develop action plans so that you can manage stressful situations.*
>
> **Alcohol or other drugs:** *There are also thoughts and behaviors that can lead us to drug and alcohol use. Some of these thoughts may be related to PTSD, but not all. You will have the opportunity to practice exploring which thoughts, people, places, and things may lead you to use drugs and alcohol. If you decide to try to stop or decrease how much you drink or use, we can practice that as well. You will practice making decisions and consider making changes in drug and alcohol use. We can practice all the techniques together and role-play so you are even more ready to test new strategies out in real life.*
>
> **Mindfulness skills:** *Mindfulness is a training of the mind to be able to concentrate better and to decrease the "noise" and constant chattering of your mind, especially upsetting thoughts and feelings. By observing your mind like a scientist watches an experiment, without judgment but with great curiosity, you*

will be able to see clearly the ways of thinking that add further stress to your life. The instant you recognize that your mind has been trapped in a story about a painful memory or has begun to worry about the future, you can choose to come back to the here and now. You will learn to develop the ability to feel whatever you are feeling, making room for the bodily sensations, feelings, and emotions that happen to show up, both pleasant and unpleasant. By bringing attention to thoughts and feelings of anxiety, fear, worry, anger, or any other feeling as best you can, you will notice that they come and go, just like clouds, and that there is no need to act on them. You can just watch them come and go, one cloud or feeling after the other, just as a spectator in a movie theater watches with curiosity what is presented. This is a first step in helping you respond to thoughts and situations that may be triggers for reacting automatically, without awareness about what is happening. Awareness through mindfulness is a way of becoming more able to respond to things in a way you want to as opposed to reacting on "automatic pilot." You, not your thoughts, become the driver of your emotional car.

In mindfulness we have some tools, or practices, to help us deal with stress and disturbing feelings. At the center of mindfulness is bringing yourself back into the present moment—by using any of the five senses; by paying attention to the breath; by feeling the sensations in your body while doing the body scan, stretching, walking, eating, or doing whatever you are doing, knowing that you are doing it, with your mind present to what you are doing.

What are senses? [Help your client identify the five senses: sight, smell, touch (body senses), taste, and sound.]

We can also learn how to "ride" a craving like a surfer riding a wave. Scientists have found that that actually helps with addictions!

All of these skills have been shown to reduce symptoms resulting from trauma or scary experiences, such as thoughts about the trauma, nightmares, high levels of stress, and even anger (if we don't want to hold on to those feelings). The skills can be very helpful in working with anxiety, fear, and even panic attacks. They can also provide you with a way to feel more balanced and have more awareness about yourself and your well-being.

Tell the client that you know you have covered a lot, and ask the following questions:

What questions do you have about what I have described?

What would you hope to be able to work on together?

Can you tell me what you understand from what I have talked about thus far?

What seems interesting?

If you decide to continue, what might be some goals you would want to work on?

Listen intentionally to what the adolescent offers or asks and reflect back what you hear. Continue to use open-ended questions, reflections, and affirmations throughout the session. This session is not only about offering information but also about building rapport and motivation for continuing—the latter is most important.

D. Weighing my options

In this step, you will weigh the pros and cons of change and assess the adolescent's motivation for change. Review **handout 3: Weighing My Options** and tables 7.1 and 7.2.

When you make a decision, make changes, or set goals, it can be helpful to think about the good things, and the not-so-good things, about making changes. I just gave you a lot of information about ways we can learn and practice together. But an important part of this is what you would like to see happen. Maybe there are changes you want to see in your life. Maybe you have some other ideas about all of this.

Let's look at the idea of coming to counseling [or therapy, coaching, or whatever other word the adolescent wishes to use]. *There are likely some pros and cons to doing that. Let's see how you might weigh that option.*

In addition to those listed on the handout, elicit from the adolescent any other pros and cons of coming to counseling.

Table 7.1 Pros and Cons of Coming to Counseling

Pros of Coming to Counseling	Cons of Coming to Counseling
• I could feel better. • I could accomplish my goals. • I could have better relationships. • I could have more energy. • I could do things better. • List any others:	• It's uncomfortable to talk about my problems. • It's hard to make changes. • It takes work to feel better. • Therapy requires time. • It feels like therapy does not help. • List any others:

This is also a way to decide whether you are ready for or interested in making any changes in your drug and alcohol use. You always have the option to weigh the pros and cons of making any change. Can we look at that as well?

In addition to those listed on handout 3, elicit from the adolescent any other pros and cons of using, reducing, or abstaining from drugs or alcohol.

Table 7.2 Pros and Cons of Using, Reducing, and Abstaining from Drugs and Alcohol

Pros of Using	Cons of Using
• I don't have to deal with my problems. • I feel more confident. • I have something to do when I am bored. • I fit in with my friends. • I have more fun at parties. • It helps me calm down and relax. • List any others:	• I feel guilty or ashamed. • I don't like the way I look and feel after I use. • It is a problem between my family and me. • It is a problem between my friends and me. • I run out of money. • I will continue to feel anxious and depressed. • I will harm my health. • I am having unprotected sex. • List any others:
Cons of Reducing or Stopping	**Pros of Reducing or Stopping**
• I will feel more depressed and/or anxious. • I won't have anything to do when I'm bored. • I won't have any way to relax. • I will have to change my social life. • I won't fit in with some friends. • I don't know if I can make changes stick. • List any others:	• I will feel more in control over my life. • I will feel good about myself. • It will improve my relationship with my family. • I will have more money. • I will have fewer problems at school. • It will make it easier to do things. • List any others:

Let's keep track of these pros and cons that you have just started to consider, which will help you to come up with some goals for change and will be part of our plan together. If you are not sure what those goals will be, we can come back to this. And you can always imagine what things you would like to change. You don't even have to know how or when yet.

Reflect back what you are hearing, including any discrepancies. For example:

On one side you say you don't want to deal with changing your drug use, but on the other side you say that using causes problems at school and home. Is that correct? What do you think about that? Tell me more.

Adolescents can present as resistant and even skeptical. Again, just ask open-ended questions, reflect, support, and roll with that resistance.

What are things you would like to be different?

What are the most important reasons you want these things to be different?

Use **handout 4: Measuring Change** as a visual aid to assist the adolescent in assessing motivation and confidence regarding change.

E. Safety plan

It will be helpful for us to go over a safety plan as we start to end today's session. We have spoken about many things today and a lot may come up over the weeks as we work together.

Review **handout 5: Substance Use and Safety Plan**, which focuses on early warning signs, whom the adolescent can call if there are any safety concerns, and how to know when help and support are needed. Go over all of the sections, even if the adolescent denies having any of these concerns (e.g., suicidal thoughts).

F. Mindful breathing

Mindful breathing is a beneficial way to end the session, to help the adolescent start his or her practice and to implement this as an initial step in every session after this one. Before this exercise, you may wish to show the adolescent the meditation bells and mention that you will be using them throughout sessions to signify the end of a meditation as well as the end of a session.

Wow, we did a lot today. In the first session we usually have to cover a bit more. I want to leave you with something that I think will be useful at home and until we meet again—it is awareness of breath practice.

Have you ever done any breathing exercises before? What was that like? Mindful breathing can be one of the most powerful tools to calm yourself whenever you are experiencing flashbacks, memories, strong emotions, panic attacks, or the impulse to be destructive to yourself or others. Breathing is always available. It goes wherever you go. Can we do a little practice now?

Exercise: Brief Mindful Breathing Practice

Place your hands at the center of the stomach or one hand on the stomach and another hand on the chest.

Feel how your belly moves out with the in-breath and moves in with the out-breath.

Whenever you notice that your mind has moved from feeling the direct sensation of the movement of the breath in your belly, notice where the mind went (school, home, a discussion with a friend, and so on) and you can bring it, gently and firmly, back to your breath.

If your mind leaves a hundred times, you can bring the attention back to the direct sensations of the breath, with a lot of compassion and patience for yourself, without giving yourself a hard time.

The breath teaches us that all is constantly changing, coming in and going out, just like the waves on the shore.

Ring the bells softly three times, indicating the end of the awareness of breath practice.

Note to clinician: Sometimes the adolescent has difficulty feeling the movement of the breath in the body and begins to "think" about the breath or to try to manipulate it. It might be helpful to invite him or her to place both hands on the stomach, or one hand on the stomach and one hand on the chest, so as to tangibly feel the movement of the breath. You can model this by placing your hands on your own stomach and tangibly feeling the breath. This exercise tends to be very grounding and can be used at any time when fear, anxiety, sadness, anger, or any other emotion is strong and the adolescent feels out of balance. Every time that you lead a mindfulness practice, it is important to take a few moments to process the experience briefly.

Process the practice that just ended:

What did you notice? Any discoveries, any challenges?

G. Inspirational reading

See appendix D for suggested selections. Rumi's "The Guest House" is often used when introducing mindfulness.

H. Assign daily practice

Assign the adolescent to read **handout 1: About the Program** and **handout 2: PTSD, Drugs, Alcohol, and the Brain** and to practice mindful breathing at home throughout the upcoming weeks.

Thank you so much for your work during this session.

I'm going to ask that you practice the awareness of breath at home; practice is the way to become comfortable in using it whenever you need to. Let's try this: twice a day, please do a three-minute awareness of breath exercise, with hands on the stomach, just as we did today.

I'm also going to give you some handouts about the different topics we discussed to review. Please look over them and we can talk about any questions you might have in the next session. Do you have any questions now?

Provide **handouts 1–5**.

I. Closing

Set up next meeting:

Let's determine a time when we can meet next.

End with loving-kindness phrases. Ask the adolescent to repeat silently the phrases that you are going to say (or to select his or her own phrases). Then, with your eyes closed or lowered, say all three of these phrases once, or select any of them to repeat if desired:

May I be safe and protected, may I have inner and outer safety. May I be happy, peaceful, and well. May all beings be happy, peaceful, and well.

Ask the adolescent to silently reflect for a moment on the meaning of the words and prepare to leave the session. Ring the bells softly three times, indicating the end of the session. Thank the adolescent for attending.

Meeting 2: Introduction to Mindfulness

The focus of this meeting is to expand upon the awareness of breath practice and introduce informal and formal mindfulness practices that can be helpful in promoting awareness to feelings, thoughts, and body responses. The mindfulness exercises are especially helpful in promoting awareness of thoughts and body reactions, which in turn enables the adolescent to make choices about healthy responses to events in his or her life. If needed, this session can be divided into two meetings to allow ample time to cover all of the material and to practice.

Meeting Preparation

Clinician Practice Formulate your full intention to be present during today's session. Whenever you notice that the participant is going into a story, or you are, remember the STOP technique: Stop and pause. Take a few moments to connect with the breath and invite the adolescent to do the same. Observe the body—if it's rigid, open and soften, notice any thoughts and emotions that are present, and escort your attention back to the breath. Proceed when both you and the adolescent feel balanced and present.

Practice the fourfold approach: 1) show up and choose to be present, 2) pay attention to what has heart and meaning, 3) tell the truth without blame or judgment, and 4) be open to outcome.

Review the guided Eating Meditation (with Raisin) script in appendix A.

Materials

- Flipchart and markers
- Copy of Weekly Rating Sheet (handout 6; see appendix B)
- Handouts 7 and 8
- Box or bowl of raisins, nuts, or small candies
- Meditation bells
- Folder of poems and quotes

Meeting 2 Outline

A. Mindful breathing or mindful stretching (5 minutes)

B. One-word check-in (2 minutes)

C. Review previous week's and today's intentions (6 minutes)

D. Weekly ratings (5 minutes)

E. Introduce informal mindfulness practice (15 minutes)

F. Introduce formal mindfulness practice (20 minutes)

G. Assign daily practice (2 minutes)

H. Closing (5 minutes)

Meeting 2 Detailed Guide

A. Mindful breathing or mindful stretching

For this first exercise, please select either the Awareness of Breath exercise provided below or one or two of the mindful movement exercises in the Mindful Standing Stretching Practice at the end of appendix A.

Exercise: Awareness of Breath

Place your hands at the center of the stomach or one hand on the stomach and another hand on the chest. Feel the expansion of the belly with the in-breath and the contraction or deflation with the out-breath.

Place your hand on your own belly and feel the contraction and expansion of the belly with the breath, noticing that the belly expands with the in-breath and contracts with the out-breath. Do this in silence, allowing the adolescent to feel the rhythmic movement of the breath. Then, continue to guide the adolescent:

Whenever you notice that the mind has moved from feeling the direct sensation of the movement of the breath in your belly, notice where the mind went (for example, school, home, a discussion with a friend) and you can escort it, gently and firmly, back to the breath.

If the mind leaves a hundred times, your task is to bring the attention back to the direct sensations of the breath, with a lot of compassion and patience for yourself, without giving yourself a hard time. Pay attention to the in-breath and the full duration of the out-breath.

Do this in silence for two minutes, allowing the adolescent and yourself to feel the beginning, middle, and end of the in-breath, the gap in between, and the out-breath. If you wish, ask the following question:

Are you in the here and now?

End with some comments about the breath, such as the following:

The breath teaches us that all is constantly changing—coming in and going out, just like the waves on the shore. The breath will be with us until the last moment that we are alive; it is always present; it is portable; we can use it as a place we can always go to, as our home base, a place to return when we feel out of balance to help us come back to the here and now. We can also allow the breath to help us.

In a moment I will ring the bells, indicating the end of this meditation. I will invite you to allow the sounds of the bells to completely disappear before you move.

After completing this (or the mindful stretching) exercise, ring the meditation bells softly three times. Process the practice that just ended:

Were there any discoveries, anything that you noticed, any challenges that you experienced while you did the mindful breathing or mindful stretching?

B. One-word check-in

Take a moment to go inward and note what you are feeling or thinking. Can you check in with one word that kind of describes what you are experiencing this moment? Can you share it with me?

Explain that these brief one-word check-ins will be used at the beginning of each session to help the adolescent gauge what he or she is experiencing in the moment, for you to get a sense of that as well, and as part of the practice of building awareness.

C. Review of previous week's and today's intentions

Review what you discussed in last week's session and any questions about the handouts. Ask whether the adolescent found time to practice the awareness of breath. Next, go over the intentions for today, written on the flipchart.

Today we are going to learn about a practice called mindfulness, which I briefly mentioned last week. But before we do that, let's discuss how things have been going.

D. Weekly ratings

Let's take a minute so you can tell me how you have been feeling lately. First, I'll just ask you a few questions about how you may have been feeling. This will help us to understand how things are going and how we should move forward.

Throughout our sessions together I am going to ask you to evaluate your alcohol or drug use and other symptoms using a 10-point scale, where 1 is the worst ever and 10 means no longer a concern.

Refer to part A of **handout 6: Weekly Rating Sheet**—also found in appendix B, for your convenience—for this part of the session, and use a new copy of the handout each week. Complete the ratings and accompanying questions, and then ask the adolescent to review and think about part B of handout 6 prior to the next session. This helps the adolescent to prepare and consider what he or she has noticed since the last session and would like to focus on in the next session.

E. Introduce informal mindfulness practice

In this section, explain how informal mindfulness practice can be useful anywhere.

Informal mindfulness practice is something that you can do in your daily life, while eating, brushing your teeth, taking a shower, doing the dishes, taking the garbage out, or walking. Any of these can be part of mindfulness practice.

We eat while we have the TV on, while we are in front of the computer, or while we are reading a book. Most of the time our mind is distracted by planning or is "hooked" by a story of something that happened earlier in the day or that is about to happen. For the most part we do not take the time to observe the color, the texture, or the temperature of the food that we eat unless it is too hot or too cold; nor do we attend to the taste or the process of chewing and swallowing. We do all of this in automatic pilot mode, which is the opposite of mindfulness.

To be mindful means to be present to what we are doing, noticing moment-by-moment every sensation that comes to us through our senses. When practicing mindfulness we notice the thoughts that cross our minds, and instead of trying to hold on to them, we just let them float away like clouds. We do the same thing with any emotion or feeling that we experience. We allow ourselves to feel the feeling in our body. If a distressing or unpleasant feeling arises, we use the breath to allow us to ride the wave of distress. We continue to feel the movement of the breath until the feeling exists less and less. In other words, it kind of fades.

What you will get better and better at is this: paying attention in a particular way, on purpose, in the present moment, and without judging yourself. Mindfulness requires bringing ourselves to be aware and to notice in the here and now. It is the gentle effort to be fully present in what we are feeling or even tasting.

Throughout the day you will have the opportunity to be present and appreciate any situation you find yourself in, whether it is pleasant or unpleasant. You have the possibility to notice the thoughts, feelings, and sensations that are present in your body when something is happening. You can really see what you are looking at, taste what you are eating, and smell the aromas and fragrances near you, as well as the unpleasant odors, with compassion and curiosity and without judgment. You can choose to become mindful from the moment you wake up, while brushing your teeth, taking a shower, eating breakfast, or walking or driving to school or work. You can choose to often take moments during the day to come back to yourself using the breath or any of your five senses to help you be in the present moment. The work of healing and self-care always happens when you are in the here and now. When you are in the here and now, it is hard to worry about the past or the future.

If you'd like, do the following breathing exercise afterwards:

Exercise: Three-Minute Awareness of Breath

1. AWARENESS: *Bring yourself into the present moment by sitting up and if possible, closing your eyes. Then ask yourself,* What do I notice right now...in thoughts...in feelings...and in my body? *Notice what is there, even if it is unwanted.*
2. GATHERING: *Then, gently redirect your full attention to breathing, to each in-breath and to each out-breath, as they follow, one after the other. Your breath can act like an anchor to bring you into the present and help you notice this moment.*
3. EXPANDING: *Now increase your awareness around your breathing. How does your whole body feel around your breath? Your chest? Your stomach area (abdomen)? Your arms? Your body?*

Explain that the Three-Minute Awareness of Breath exercise provides a way to step out of automatic pilot mode and reconnect with the present moment. Refer to **handout 7: Breathing and Mindfulness**, which the adolescent can review at home. If you wish, you can present other practices such as mindful standing stretches and mindful walking, keeping in mind the adolescent's own mobility, capabilities, and preferences. You can use the text that follows to introduce these exercises, and the relevant scripts in appendix A to facilitate each practice.

Exercise: Mindful Standing Stretches

Stretches are a very good way to relieve the tension that tends to store up in the body. We all have areas of the body where we tend to hold stress. For most of us, the neck and shoulders, the forehead and chin, the hands and fingers, the stomach, the center of the chest, and the lower back are areas where we feel stress. By allowing the body to move with awareness, we can release tension and release some of that stress from our body.

Exercise: Mindful Walking

You will have plenty of opportunity to practice this tool of awareness in your day-to-day life. In school going from one classroom to another, walking or returning from school, in stores, at the park, at the mall, or wherever you find yourself, see if you can place your entire attention on the sensations happening in the soles of your feet or any other part of the body. Usually when we walk, we allow the mind to go into planning, worrying, end-of-the-world thinking, assumptions, mind reading, or regrets. Or, we might just be talking on the cell phone or listening to music. This exercise allows us to bring the mind to where the body is and to feel more "in" our body.

F. Introduce formal mindfulness practice

There are also formal mindful meditations that you can use. There are audio recordings of several meditations I can share with you, as MP3 files you can save to your computer or put on your phone. [You can download these files to distribute to clients at http://www.newharbinger.com/31335.] *Formal practice consists of those times that you dedicate to listen to the audio or to do the practice on your own if you have memorized it. The formal practice is best when performed in a safe and relaxing environment, where there are minimal interruptions from other people or phones. You can perform it lying down, standing, or sitting up. It is best to schedule a time to do it, instead of hoping that you will remember to do it.*

The work of mindfulness is to become aware of our automatic reactions by stopping to observe them as clearly as possible, with curiosity. Then we are able to respond and make a different choice, instead of moving immediately to our usual reaction—what's known as automatic pilot.

Stress without awareness leads us to react automatically. We may even do things we don't really want to do or that we will regret later.

Stress with awareness of thoughts, emotions, and bodily sensations helps us respond. When we respond with awareness, then we have choice.

We will review and practice some formal mindfulness practices that can help you focus on awareness. They are called formal just because they are full meditations that can be guided, rather than informal mindfulness practices that are about being more mindful in things you do every day, like eating or walking.

Exercise: Guided Eating Meditation (Formal Practice)

Use the Eating Meditation (with Raisin) script presented in appendix A as a guide. After the practice, process the experience using inquiry for a few moments, as follows:

Any challenges? Any discoveries? What did you notice? Have you eaten raisins this way before? How do you normally eat raisins?

Let the adolescent answer and reflect his or her answers back. You can supplement what was said or offer something that was omitted.

Note to clinician: Eating mindfully and "knowing" that we are eating are different. In order to be mindful we have to purposely be aware of eating. If you are mindfully eating then you are really aware of the process of eating. You are really noticing when you use all of your senses: taste, smell, sight, hearing, and touch. When you notice your mind wandering and notice that your mind is no longer present to the process of eating, you purposefully bring it back, without giving yourself a hard time, paying attention to your chewing or swallowing.

Highlight the fact that we tend to eat on automatic pilot mode, not really tasting what we are eating, observing the colors, or experiencing the texture, fragrance, temperature, and other aspects. Encourage the adolescent to practice eating even a few bites this week in an aware and present way as it was just presented.

Exercise: Brief Body Scan

Lead this exercise by first having the adolescent bring awareness to sensations in the entire body.

How does your body feel at this moment? Is it heavy or light? Is there a feeling of tiredness? Are you holding tension in the neck, shoulders, or face?

See if you can sense the sensations of contact of the sitting bones against the chair, or the back making contact with the back of the chair, or the contact that the hands are making with each other or the legs.

Feel the breath in your belly. You may want to place your hands on your belly. Sense the expansion of the belly with the in-breath, and the contraction or deflation with the out-breath.

Move your awareness down the legs to the feet. What are you sensing in your feet at this moment? You might choose to stamp your feet to heighten sensation in the feet. Sense the contact with the floor, sensations in the toes, in the soles of the feet, in the skin, sensations of temperature, or tingling.

Then move to sensations in the ankles and the legs, exploring with curiosity any sensations present.

You might invite the adolescent to bring one leg up and circle the foot in one direction, and then flex and point the foot. Continue with the whole body, or if there is only time to do the leg, just finish there. Longer variations of this exercise are provided in appendix A (Seated Body Scan and Seated Body Scan Interspersed with Mindful Movement), the latter of which might be helpful for adolescents who have a hard time sitting due to restlessness.

Process the exercise, asking the following questions:

What did you notice during that meditation? What did you notice about your thoughts, feelings, and sensations in your body?

Practicing helps a lot. If you forget to do it for a while, no regrets—just start again.

Slowly, and gradually, you will also learn how to listen mindfully to the messages your body gives you, so the body can be used as a "tool" to get out of states of mind that make you feel unhappy. We usually use the body as a means of transporting ourselves from one place to another, and we do anything in order not to feel the stomach going into a knot, the heart beating at the speed of light, or that restless, crawling-out-of-your-skin feeling you get when you're anxious or craving something. By practicing the body scan, which is an exploration into the moment-to-moment experiences of the body, we begin to be more present to ourselves and more aware of our posture. By allowing yourself to feel your emotions and your body, and to witness your thoughts with curiosity, you can choose actions and behaviors that will help you grow, develop self-confidence, and move in the direction you would like to move in your life.

But there are some principles to all this...

Discuss the following principles and explore the adolescent's responses:

Not judging: *Witnessing and observing what is happening or what you are thinking without judging it as bad or good. We can be quick to judge ourselves; but sometimes you can say, "It just is." When you happen to be in a judging mood, just notice what is happening with compassion for yourself. Know that we learn at a very young age to judge ourselves. We may even begin to judge ourselves for judging!*

Patience: *Allowing things to unfold or become in their time, being patient with yourself and others. We don't have to rush anything; like a plant needs time to grow, you also need time to grow and learn.*

Beginner's mind: *Seeing things as if for the first time; creating possibility for seeing things in a new way; letting yourself have more moments where you say, "Hey, I never thought of that."*

Trust: *Trusting yourself, which is central to helping yourself feel better. Can you trust yourself?*

Nonstriving: *Not focusing on winning, losing, what the outcome will be, or achievement. You still try your best, but you believe you can learn from both winning and losing.*

Acceptance: *Being open to seeing and recognizing things as they are. It does not mean approval; it just means seeing things for what they are.*

Letting be: *Allowing thoughts or feelings to be there while not trying to "unpack" them or make sense of the content or reason for them. When we start paying attention to our inner thoughts, we discover that there are some thoughts and feelings that the mind wants to hold on to because they are pleasant, and others that the mind wants to get rid of because they are unpleasant. If you observe your mind holding on tightly to either keeping or rejecting thoughts or feelings, see if it is possible to let go of the grasping. It is as if you can imagine that these strong thoughts are balloons. You can look at each balloon to see its color or shape and see what its message is, but you can also let it go and let it fly away. It is okay.*

Gentleness: *Showing tenderness. It is not being passive or weak; it just means being gentle with ourselves.*

Empathy: *Feeling and understanding another person's situation, perspectives, emotions, actions, and reactions, and communicating this to the person—putting ourselves in another person's shoes.*

Generosity: *Giving within a context of love and compassion, without worrying about what you will gain. It is giving without focus on what you will get in return.*

Gratitude: *Appreciating and being thankful for the present moment.*

Loving-kindness: *Having forgiveness and unconditional love...especially for yourself.*

How do you feel about these principles? Are some harder than others for you? Which ones do you feel more comfortable with and why? What might help?

G. Assign daily practice

Remind the adolescent that the mindfulness meditation audio recording is available to assist with practice at home. Assign practice of the body scan at least once during the week as well as one of the informal mindfulness practices, for example when eating or walking each day. Ask the client to read **handout 8: Mindfulness Practices** at home to review the material covered in today's session.

H. Closing

End with three loving-kindness phrases (and, if time allows, a poem or a quote). Ring the bells softly three times and thank the adolescent for attending the session.

Meeting 3: Psychoeducation Part I—PTSD

This therapy session focuses on psychoeducation, and covers the core symptoms of PTSD and its associated emotional and interpersonal challenges. It is intended to help identify these issues for the adolescent. It is also an opportunity for the clinician to learn the perspective and experiences of the adolescent regarding these concerns. Finally, it is a time for the adolescent to begin to name and further understand some of his or her own challenges, and it provides an opportunity for you to offer reflective and mindful listening.

Meeting Preparation

Clinician Practice To prepare for this session, remember to use the fourfold approach and try to avoid being carried by the story; instead focus on witnessing and remaining in the present moment. Practice the Three-Minute Awareness of Breath exercise to moderate moments of low energy or anxiety and to ground your presence in the moment as a preparation for witnessing what will arise in the session.

Practice the body scan on a regular basis to be able to guide others from your own awareness and practice.

Review the key information about PTSD that is presented below, but use the handouts to help facilitate open-ended questioning regarding the adolescent's experience.

Materials

- Flipchart and markers
- Copy of Weekly Rating Sheet (handout 6)
- Handouts 9–15
- Meditation bells
- Folder of poems and quotes

Meeting 3 Outline

A. Mindful stretching or body scan (5 minutes)

B. One-word check-in (2 minutes)

C. Review previous week's and today's intentions (5 minutes)

D. Weekly ratings (5 minutes)

E. Impact of stressful events and trauma (30–35 minutes)

F. Assign daily practice (5 minutes)

G. Closing (5 minutes)

Meeting 3 Detailed Guide

A. Mindful stretching or body scan

Please select one or two mindful movement exercises from the Mindful Standing Stretching Practice at the end of appendix A, or proceed with the body scan meditation, as discussed below. You introduced a brief body scan practice in chapter 2; this week, you can choose to guide the adolescent in a full body scan meditation. This meditation can gradually enable the adolescent to be present in his or her body instead of living only in the mind. You can explain the meditation to the adolescent using some of the following points:

- It can be helpful in learning to feel physical sensations with a sense of exploration, with kindness toward ourselves, and in a nonjudgmental way.
- The body scan is a tool to bring us to the present moment because what we sense in our body happens in this moment.
- It helps us notice and experience the emotions that arise during the exercise (frustration, boredom, anger, anxiety, fear, worry, sadness, excitement, happiness) in a gentle and open way.
- It allows us to observe clearly that thoughts and emotions are not permanent; just like clouds, they arrive, stay for a while, and then disappear. It teaches us that we do not need to "do" anything with our thoughts or emotions—just witness them and feel them.
- Lastly, it helps us to realize that there are feelings inside of us that can help and are always available to us such as joy, calmness, unconditional love, forgiveness, patience, wisdom, strength, approval, and recognition. All we need to do is stop, breathe slowly, and quietly connect with these feelings and our senses.

Find a rhythm that works for you when you guide the adolescent in this exercise. Try to speak slowly and do the body scan yourself when you are guiding. Avoid using a commanding voice; instead, be invitational in your approach. The body scan may be performed while seated, standing, lying down, or even walking. It can be done slowly and deliberately, or in two or three minutes, just feeling sensations in the entire body and refreshing the body with the breath. There is not a "right posture" to do the body scan—what is important is to have the intention to be as attentive as possible, moment-to-moment, to the changing sensations, thoughts, and emotions arising, staying for a while, and passing away.

Two scripts of the Seated Body Scan are included in appendix A; use either script or a combination of both to guide this body scan meditation. Or create an alternative one involving standing or walking.

B. One-word check-in

Were there any discoveries, anything that you noticed, any challenges you experienced while you did the meditation? Take a moment to go inward and note what you are feeling or thinking. Can you check in and find one word that kind of describes what you are feeling right now in this moment?

C. Review previous week's and today's intentions

Review what was discussed the week before, including the brief body scan and informal mindfulness practices, and ask if the adolescent has any questions about the handouts or practices. Next, discuss today's intentions, written on the flipchart.

D. Weekly ratings

Let's take a minute as usual so you can tell me how you have been feeling lately. First, I'll just ask you a few questions about how you may have been feeling. This will help us to understand how things are going and how we should move forward.

Refer to part A of **handout 6: Weekly Rating Sheet**—also found in appendix B as well as the downloadable workbook, for your convenience—and proceed through the ratings and questions with the client. Afterwards, ask the client to review and think about part B of handout 6 prior to the next session.

E. Impact of stressful events and trauma

We have already started talking about being aware of what we feel in our bodies, our emotions, and even what we may think. We have also mentioned the ideas of stress and post-traumatic stress. I would like to talk to with you about this, as sometimes knowing and understanding what we are experiencing can be helpful. Maybe you have heard a few things about post-traumatic stress disorder or PTSD.

What have you heard about this?

Post-traumatic stress disorder, or PTSD, is a disorder that can develop in children, adolescents, or adults as a result of directly experiencing, witnessing, or being confronted with a single traumatic life event or a period of prolonged stress due to a traumatic experience.

One-time traumatic events may include experiencing or witnessing a serious car or pedestrian accident; major falls; burns or other types of accidents; violent crimes including being attacked or beaten up; dog attacks; natural and man-made disasters such as fires, floods, chemical explosions, or cyclones; undergoing emergency medical treatments; being diagnosed with a life-threatening medical condition such as cancer; or being confronted with family members or close peers who have suffered from a life-threatening situation.

Prolonged traumatic events include repeatedly experiencing or witnessing—over weeks, months, or years—physical and/or sexual assault or abuse, or living or working in regions affected by war or violence.

Traumatic events that can cause PTSD involve a potential threat to one's life or a threat of injury to oneself or other people. Research has shown that up to 40 percent of adolescents have experienced at least one traumatic life event, and about 80 percent of individuals will have experienced at least one traumatic event in their lifetime.

However, not all adolescents who experience traumatic events will develop PTSD, and not everyone who has trauma has all of the symptoms of PTSD; they may have some symptoms and not others. They may have some problems with school, or with work, or with family. They may use substances to forget or to feel better—at least for a little while.

What do you think about what I am saying so far? How do you feel about talking about it?

Consider guiding the adolescent in the Three-Minute Awareness of Breath exercise to refocus before moving on to discuss the following symptoms. Refer to **handout 9: Reexperiencing the Event**, **handout 10: Avoidance**, and **handout 11: My Signs of Stress**.

Reexperiencing: *People often find themselves reliving the traumatic event(s). A common way you might reexperience an event is by just starting to think about or remember what happened to you, even if you don't want to. All of a sudden the memory feels real and you may get anxious, as if it is actually happening again.*

Avoidance: *It is very common for people to avoid people, things, or places that remind them of an upsetting event. We avoid so we don't have to have all those difficult feelings. Sometimes it's automatic: you don't have to tell yourself,* Don't think about that—*you just do it automatically.*

Body reactions to stress: *These are reactions that make your body feel really tense. You might have problems sleeping, feel jumpy or jittery, get angry, or have trouble concentrating. You may feel like you're always looking over your shoulder to make sure you're safe.*

Summarize:

When a person has all three kinds of symptoms or reactions, they have PTSD.

Are any of these things you experience or have experienced?

Which are the worst? Which come up most often? When?

Try to elicit examples from the adolescent's own experiences. Encourage relaxation and mindful breathing practice if the adolescent becomes tense; discuss his or her experience of that practice in the midst of thinking about some of these issues. Continue the discussion by referring to **handout 12: Coping with Stress** and **handout 13: Emotions Associated with PTSD** and addressing the following common symptoms:

Nervousness and fear: *While it's common to be afraid after a traumatic event because there was danger, with PTSD, some people continue to feel afraid in situations that aren't really dangerous. For example, a boy is bitten by a dog, and every time he hears a dog bark he feels like he is going to get bitten again.*

There are some other types of feelings that you might have after experiencing traumatic and stressful things. They are not always related to having PTSD but can be a reaction to traumatic and stressful situations anyway.

Sadness and depression: *With PTSD, people often feel less interested in things, have a hard time having fun, or feel hopeless and think about hurting themselves. Do you ever feel sad or depressed? How do you feel or act when you are depressed?*

Guilt and shame: *With PTSD, people blame themselves in some way for what happened. They feel it was their fault, that it happened because they deserved it or did something wrong. What things tend to make you feel guilty?*

Anger: *With PTSD, people can feel angry about all kinds of things: people who did something to them, people who didn't keep them safe, or just angry with no one in particular. Sometimes people feel angry with themselves. What are some things, people, or places that make you angry?*

F. Assign daily practice

Introduce the adolescent to **handout 14: Pleasant Events Calendar** and **handout 15: Unpleasant Events Calendar** to be completed at home. You can use the partially filled-in copies of each chart on the following pages, along with the script provided.

As part of your practice this week, try to become aware of both pleasant and unpleasant events, thoughts, and feelings that you experience. We will look at an example to help you. Try to fill the calendar in with some events this week and note and include what you felt and experienced in that moment of the event. Again, you are just experimenting with becoming more aware of what you feel and when...and maybe even why.

Table 7.3 Pleasant Events Calendar

Day	What was the experience?	What pleasant feelings were you aware of while the event was happening?	How did your body feel during this experience?	What mood, thoughts, and feelings accompanied this event?	What thoughts are in your mind now as you write about the event?
	Example: *I received a letter of acceptance to my favorite vocational school.*	*I wanted to jump up and down and to immediately call my parents and my boyfriend.*	*I was smiling, my body felt light, my voice was happy. Energetic.*	*Happiness, excitement, enthusiasm.*	*My life will change. So happy to have this opportunity to do what I want to do.*
Monday					
Tuesday					
Wednesday					

Table 7.4 Unpleasant Events Calendar

Day	What was the experience?	What unpleasant feelings were you aware of while the event was happening?	How did your body feel during this experience?	What mood, thoughts, and feelings accompanied this event?	What thoughts are in your mind now as you write about the event?
	Example: *I failed my math test.*	*It was as if someone had hit me in the stomach.*	*My shoulders went up, my chest was contracted, my stomach was in a knot.*	*I was angry and sad. I was upset for the rest of the day.*	*My mom will be disappointed in me.*
Monday					
Tuesday					
Wednesday					

After discussing the pleasant and unpleasant events calendars, invite the adolescent to start becoming familiar with the formal mindfulness meditations by listening to one or more of the audio-recorded meditations at home this week.

G. Closing

End with three loving-kindness phrases (and, if time allows, a poem or a quote). Ring the bells softly three times and thank the participant for attending the session.

Meeting 4: Psychoeducation Part II—Risk Behaviors and Drug and Alcohol Triggers

The overarching goal of this session is to identify how PTSD and risk behaviors, including using drugs and alcohol, can be linked to one another, and to explicitly use motivational enhancement to identify and promote readiness for change. You and the client can return to these exercises at other times during the course of treatment whenever the client is considering making changes. The session helps the adolescent continue to build awareness of feelings and thoughts as well as the practice of mindfulness.

Meeting Preparation

Clinician Practice Formulate your intention to be present to the body (i.e., embodied). Whenever you notice that the participant is going into a story, or you are, take a few moments and practice the fourfold approach: show up and choose to be present, pay attention to what has heart and meaning, tell the truth without blame or judgment, and be open to outcome.

Materials

- Flipchart and markers
- Copy of Weekly Rating Sheet (handout 6)
- Handouts 16–18

- Meditation bells
- Folder of poems and quotes

Meeting 4 Outline

A. Formal mindfulness practice (18 minutes)

B. One-word check-in (2 minutes)

C. Review previous week's and today's intentions (5 minutes)

D. Weekly ratings (5 minutes)

E. Awareness of choices (10 minutes)

F. Problems linked to PTSD (10 minutes)

G. Assign daily practice (5 minutes)

H. Closing (5 minutes)

Meeting 4 Detailed Guide

A. Formal mindfulness practice

Choose any you would like from appendix A or ask for the adolescent's preference. After the mindfulness practice, process it with the adolescent.

B. One-word check-in

Were there any discoveries, anything that you noticed, any challenges you experienced while we did the meditation? Take a moment to go inward and note what you are feeling or thinking. Can you check in with one word that kind of describes what you are experiencing this moment?

C. Review previous week's and today's intentions

Review what you discussed the week before, including the formal and informal mindfulness practices, and ask if the adolescent has any questions about **handouts 14 and 15** on pleasant and unpleasant events. What were some of the experiences noted? Was the adolescent able to note what he or she felt or thought during those experiences? Also inquire about the practice at home:

Were you able to make time at home this week to do the formal practice with the audio recordings? How about the informal practice?

Ask the client about what happened at home this week. Next, discuss today's intentions, written on the flipchart.

D. Weekly ratings

Let's take a minute as usual so you can tell me how you have been feeling lately. First, I'll just ask you a few questions about how you may have been feeling. This will help us to understand how things are going and how we should move forward.

Refer to part A of **handout 6: Weekly Rating Sheet**—included in appendix B, for convenience—and proceed through the ratings and questions with the client. Afterwards, ask the client to review and think about part B of handout 6 prior to the next session.

E. Awareness of choices

Read "Autobiography in Five Chapters," by Portia Nelson, included here and in **handout 16**. This poem gives us an example of how we can become aware of patterns in our lives and how by doing so we can make different choices. Discuss how mindfulness can help us be aware of choices we can make and be fully aware of what is happening. Go over the questions that follow the poem.

This is a true story, but it is also the story of our lives when we are not mindful enough.

Autobiography in Five Chapters, by Portia Nelson

1. I walk down the street.
   There is a deep hole in the sidewalk.
   I fall in.
   I am lost… I am hopeless.
   It isn't my fault.
   It takes forever to find a way out.

2. I walk down the same street.
   There is a deep hole in the ground.
   I pretend I don't see it.
   I fall in again.
   I can't believe I'm in the same place.
   But it isn't my fault.
   It still takes a long time to get out.

3. I walk down the same street.
   There is a deep hole in the sidewalk
   I see it is there.
   I still fall in… it's a habit.
   My eyes are open.
   I know where I am.
   It's my fault.
   I get out immediately.

4. I walk down the same street.
   There is a deep hole in the sidewalk.
   I walk around it.

5. I walk down another street.

We all have triggers of one sort or another, things in which we get caught up time after time—reacting in the same ways (or falling into the same hole). Before these things can be changed we need to see them clearly.

Review the following questions in session, and ask the adolescent to ponder the questions on the handout at home.

1. What does the story in the poem tell us about experiences and choices?
2. What does it tell us about automatic reactions we all can have?
3. How does this relate to your own story?
4. What does it tell us about how awareness can help us?
5. Let's think for a moment—what causes you to fall in the same "hole" over and over again?
6. What does it feel like both in your body and in your mind before you fall in the same hole and when you are in the hole?
7. How do you treat yourself when you are in the hole? How do you treat other people?
8. What would walking down another street look like?
9. What would be different about how you are handling your life and relationships?
10. Who has the power to determine which street you walk down?

F. Problems linked to PTSD

I'd like to talk a little about some problems that can be linked to PTSD: lack of trust, heavy drug or alcohol use, and risky behaviors such as unsafe sex, disordered eating, and fighting. It's common for people with PTSD to have difficulty in relationships.

Go over **handout 17: Trouble Getting Along with Others**, which pertains to PTSD-associated problems. Ask what the adolescent identifies with regarding these.

We will also talk about what you consider might be helpful to change in your life and what you don't want to change right now.

In an earlier session we learned about symptoms that can sometimes arise after trauma or other stressful situations. Some people with stress symptoms do other kinds of risky things, such as getting involved in fights, cutting, having unsafe sex, engaging in unhealthy eating habits such as binging and purging or taking diet pills, or using drugs and alcohol.

Drugs and alcohol can be something we use or overuse when we experience certain triggers or are in specific types of situations. They are like a hole we tend to fall in, like the one in "Autobiography of Five Chapters."

Discuss triggers, the people, places, and things that might provoke us into craving or using substances. Refer to **handout 18: Risk Behaviors and Drug and Alcohol Triggers**. Go over the general categories that follow.]**General Categories of Triggers for Drug and Alcohol Use:**

- Feelings (angry, depressed, happy, sad)
- Physical state (relaxed, anxious, tense)
- Being around certain other people
- Availability (the drugs were right in front of me)
- Being in certain places
- Activities (work, sports, parties, sex)
- Thoughts

Ask and discuss the following questions related to triggers and drug or alcohol use:

When are you most likely to drink? Who is around?

When are you most likely to use drugs? Who is around?

What do you tend to think before you use or drink?

Briefly describe one of your high-risk or trigger situations for using drugs or alcohol.

Describe the type of consequences usually associated with the situation. Consider both positive and negative consequences.

Is there anything you wish you could change or try differently in these situations? Would it be okay if we looked at what you could do to make that change?

Ask the adolescent to respond to the following statements:

The changes I want to make are...

The most important reasons I want to make these changes are...

The steps I plan to take in changing are...

The ways other people can help me are...

I will know that my plan is working if...

Some things that could interfere with my plan are...

The ways that I can address these barriers are...

Ask the adolescent to consider one change mentioned above and answer the following questions about it:

On a scale of 1 to 10, how important is making that change?

On a scale of 1 to 10, how confident are you that you can make that change?

What could help you feel more confident?

G. Assign daily practice

Again, the mindfulness meditation audio is available to help you practice at home. Practice a formal mindfulness meditation at least once at home this week as well as one of the informal mindfulness practices each day, for example when eating or walking. Try completing at least one step toward the change you said you wanted to make during this week.

Note: you can return to **handout 4: Measuring Change** and **handout 5: Substance Use and Safety Plan** during any session if it seems that there is a shift in the adolescent's readiness for change. Today, read the following list of steps to the adolescent, indicating that these are the six key steps that will assist him or her in making change:

1. Remind yourself of the reasons you want to change.
2. Think about your past attempts at quitting, if any. What worked? What didn't?
3. Set specific, measurable goals, such as a quit date or limits on your drug use.
4. Remove reminders of the substance from your home.
5. Tell friends and family that you're quitting and ask for their support.
6. Be aware of your triggers and sense when you are craving.

H. Closing

End with three loving-kindness phrases (and, if time allows, a poem or a quote). Let the adolescent choose the phrases! Ring the bells softly three times and thank the participant for attending the session.

Meeting 5: Managing Triggers, Cravings, and Urges

This session focuses on coping strategies for cravings and urges and further encourages the use of skills that have already been discussed (mindfulness, managing cravings or distressing feelings). You will help the adolescent elicit new ideas for managing cravings and urges, which can include adding other support people, music, media, spirituality, and any other resources. The aim is to lead the adolescent to consider, specify, and articulate a recovery and relapse prevention plan when he or she is ready. You will continue to explore the variety of triggers that may exist—trauma-related or otherwise—and invite the adolescent to role-play with you difficult scenarios that may present a risk for relapse in order to prepare for these situations as they come up over time.

Meeting Preparation

Clinician Practice Use the fourfold approach (described in meeting 2). Rather than being carried by the story, try to focus on and offer the space for witnessing, remaining in the present moment. Practice the Three-Minute Awareness of Breath exercise to help moderate moments of low energy or anxiety and to focus your presence in the moment as a preparation for witnessing the adolescent without judgment and with compassion.

Materials

- Flipchart and markers
- Copy of Weekly Rating Sheet (handout 6)
- Handouts 19–21
- Meditation bells
- Folder of poems and quotes

Meeting 5 Outline

A. Formal mindfulness practice (10 minutes)

B. One-word check-in (2 minutes)

C. Review previous week's and today's intentions (5 minutes)

D. Weekly ratings (5 minutes)

E. Cravings, triggers, and drug and alcohol use (10)

F. Riding the Roller Coaster (18)

G. Assign daily practice (5 minutes)

H. Closing (2 minutes)

Meeting 5 Detailed Guide

A. Formal mindfulness practice

Choose a mindfulness practice, or ask if the adolescent has a preference, and guide the adolescent in the meditation. Afterwards, process the meditation by asking the following questions:

Was there anything new that you noticed? Any challenges or difficulties you experienced while you did the meditation? What did you experience in your body? What were the thoughts and emotions that came up?

B. One-word check-in

Take a moment to go inward and note what you are feeling or thinking. Can you check in with one word that kind of describes what you are experiencing or feeling right now?

C. Review previous week's and today's intentions

Review what you discussed the week before, including the formal and informal mindfulness practices and psychoeducation component, and see if the adolescent was able to initiate any step toward change on the plan from last week. Consider whether there is a need to explore it from different angles, or for the adolescent to show compassion or kindness toward him- or herself in looking at this.

What were some of the challenges? What was easy or helpful? What are some other ways to look at the issue or other steps that might be helpful? How do you feel about trying this step?

Next, inquire about the practice at home. Did he or she find time to do it? What happened? Were there any aftereffects?

Review today's intentions, written on the flipchart.

D. Weekly ratings

Let's take a minute as usual so you can tell me how you have been feeling lately. First, I'll just ask you a few questions about how you may have been feeling. This will help us to understand how things are going and how we should move forward.

Refer to part A of **handout 6: Weekly Rating Sheet** (also found in appendix B), and proceed through the ratings and questions with the client. Afterwards, ask the client to review and think about part B of that handout prior to the next session.

E. Craving, triggers, and drug and alcohol use

Jon Kabat-Zinn (1990) tells the story of catching monkeys in a certain area of India. To introduce the concepts in this segment, you can share a version of the story included below:

The Monkey Story: Illustrating Letting Go

> They say that in India there is a particularly clever way of catching monkeys. As the story goes, hunters will cut a hole in a coconut that is just big enough for a monkey to put its hand through. Then they will drill two smaller holes in the other end, pass a wire through, and secure the coconut to the base of a tree. Then they put a banana inside the coconut and hide. The monkey comes down, puts its hand in and takes hold of the banana. The hole is crafted so that the open hand can go in but the fist cannot get out. All the monkey has to do to be free is to let go of the banana. But it seems most monkeys don't let go. (Kabat-Zinn, 1990/2013, p. 39)

What is interesting is that despite our intelligence, we act very similarly to the monkeys in the story. Even though someone or something is creating a problem for us in our life, we often have trouble letting go of that habit or pattern of interaction. The work of mindfulness allows us to see clearly which banana we are holding on to that is keeping us stuck. When we begin to pay attention to how our mind functions, we begin to see clearly that there are certain habits we have that are not helping us any longer. If they are pleasant we try to prolong them, and if they are unpleasant we want to push them away, ignore them, deny them, or at times to conquer them. All of these are tiring after a while. Noticing how it feels to hold on and how it feels to let go, and the consequences of the two even for short periods of time, can be very helpful.

There are things that can lead us to being unable to let go, or to desiring things like drugs and alcohol despite their cost to us. These are things we call triggers, which we discussed last week, and also cravings. Triggers and cravings are interesting words. This is what they mean:

Triggers are people, places, things, and situations that can lead us to drink or use drugs. Everyone is different, so everyone has a different set of triggers. One common trigger is seeing someone who is drunk or high. Other common ones are getting paid, being really happy, having a bad memory, reaching the end of a hard day or week, getting into an argument with someone, and even being bored.

What do you think your triggers are?

Cravings and urges refer to a strong desire to use a particular substance—drugs of abuse such as cocaine, or foods such as chocolate. A craving is a major factor in relapse or continued substance abuse. It can feel different for different people. It can be triggered by memories, people, places, or things, or it can come like a wave out of the blue. It is often a passing thing. It does not have to lead to actually using—it will pass.

Do you experience cravings?

What do cravings or urges feel like to you?

As for relapse and recovery, relapse means that after not using substances such as drugs or alcohol for a while, maybe a few days or weeks or more, you then start to use them again.

Recovery is a period of maintaining abstinence from—or not using—substances by practicing relapse prevention, which we will discuss.

Discuss and practice some of the strategies below with the adolescent. Note that it may be hard for you to illustrate the practices fully in a session if there is not a current trigger or strong feeling. But walk through it and encourage practice.

There are tools to help you manage triggers and cravings and keep you from automatically reacting or using substances. These can help you move toward recovery and relapse prevention by at least giving you the chance to make a choice. Two strategies we will talk about are the STOP technique and the stop light metaphor.

Refer to **handout 19: STOP Technique and Stop Light Metaphor**, also found in appendix B. First, introduce the STOP technique, which is a brief way to develop awareness in daily events and slow down automatic reactions and behaviors.

Whenever you notice yourself getting off-balance or reacting in an automatic way to a situation,

Stop, or pause;

Take a breath;

Observe, open, soften;

Proceed when you feel centered.

Next, you may wish to point out to the adolescent that one way to remember the steps of the STOP technique is through the stop light metaphor. Explain the idea of paying attention to our emotions, just as we do to the traffic signals, to determine whether to proceed or not and when we need to hit the brakes.

Exercise: The Stop Light

The stop light metaphor, which is slightly different from the STOP technique, is also something that you can use any time, in just a matter of seconds. It helps you calm down before you react automatically and do something you might regret. It can help you pause and make a choice about whether or not to use drugs or drink when you have a trigger. It can help you avoid blowing up at someone when you are getting angry. It can be really handy. It goes like this:

Red Light: *Stop. Don't react just yet.*

Yellow Light: *Take caution. Notice if you are out of balance—for example, are you angry or feeling like you are getting out of control? Breathe. Don't act. Don't react. Put on your brakes. Continue to breathe mindful breaths until you find that the emotions are calming down. Only when you feel balanced and ready do you move to the green light.*

Green Light: *Proceed. Respond with a helpful action you can take in that moment.*

F. Riding the Roller Coaster

Here you'll introduce the roller coaster meditation, which will help the adolescent work mindfully with his or her emotions and cravings.

Exercise: Riding the Roller Coaster of Cravings and Urges

The purpose of this exercise is to learn to be with the experiences of cravings and urges with "affectionate curiosity"—a kind of curiosity that is compassionate, nonjudgmental, gentle, and at the same time focused. The aim is to try to see with clarity what is behind what you are feeling, what is below the surface and at the root of the craving. It is being interested in finding the cause and not necessarily the symptoms. Is the desire to use due to sad emotions or happy emotions? The need to fit in with your peers? The need for freedom? Or simply to try something different, exciting, and risky?

Our emotions, desires, and senses can all peak and plunge. Sometimes it can feel like we are on a roller coaster.

The first step is to know that you are out of center, unbalanced, and in danger of relapsing. Start to pay close attention to see what is happening as clearly as possible: Where are you? Who is there? What is happening? Did anyone do anything to trigger you? If so, what was it? Did something that happened trigger a disturbing thought or emotion from your past? Check in with your body to see if there is a feeling in the pit of the stomach, or anywhere else. How is your breath: is it shallow and fast? Do you feel like you are crawling out of your skin? Are you sad, frustrated, angry, frightened? The invitation here is to notice, as best possible, the bodily sensations, emotions, feelings, and thoughts that you are having, not wanting to change anything, but just to see clearly.

After assessing clearly what is happening at that moment, find a place of safety or refuge, either internally or externally. To do this internally, if you have been practicing awareness of breath meditation, the in-breath and the out-breath can be a place to focus your attention, concentrating on one of the five senses (hearing, seeing, touching, smelling, tasting) or walking mindfully can create this place of refuge. To do this externally, find someone to talk with who you know will be helpful.

The approach to guiding this experience is similar in fashion to guiding the mindful eating practice with the raisins, nuts, or small candies. It is about seeing everything that can possibly be seen—to look at the experience with beginner's eyes, with a nonjudgmental attitude, and with acceptance.

If you wish, you can use the body scan as a model. The detailed nature of the body scan—paying attention to the sensations in the big toe, the little toe, the toes in between, the spaces between the toes, sensations of temperature or moisture in the skin, and so on—can serve effectively in the process of seeing. See the Seated Body Scan and Seated Body Scan Interspersed with Mindful Movement scripts in appendix A.

Rather than falling into the usual pattern of reacting or resisting, the intention here is to become intimate with what arises when cravings or urges are present: Where do you feel it in your body? Can you observe the wave like cravings and urges—appearing, reaching a peak, and washing away? What do you say to yourself when you have a strong urge or a craving? Can you notice the thoughts that arise? Maybe those of anticipation or desperation: I cannot stand it one more moment, I am going to fall apart, *or* This experience will be great. *What emotions are present? Can you feel where the particular emotions are felt in your body? It is also useful to question how you treat yourself and how you treat others when you have a strong urge or craving.*

Go over **handout 20: Rethinking Your Thoughts About Using Substances** and **handout 21: Triggering Thoughts, Feelings, and Experiences** and consider the following questions and ideas. You can come back to these strategies anytime in later sessions.

Let's examine some common thoughts that young people like you may have that are related to drug use. Do you sometimes think some of these? What are some alternative thoughts or ways of seeing these things?

Even if you're not sure you need to change, keep track of your triggers for substance use in a diary, and bring that diary in so we can discuss these and continue to come up with coping strategies. This will give you more information about the role of substance use in your life, the types of triggers you experience, and how you can overcome them.

What strategies or changes can help you in these situations to not use drugs or alcohol? Write some here [on handout 21] *and let's practice what you may say or do in these situations.*

If there are situations involving people who lead you to use drugs when you don't want to, we can do a role-play and practice how to say no. [See role-play steps in appendix C.]

When you are craving drugs, alcohol, or another risky behavior, consider the following:

If you drank to relax and cope with stress, then you need alternative, new ways to relax and reduce stress. Some of the relaxation and mindfulness techniques we have learned might help. Doing something else that you enjoy, like listening to music, can also help. Have your favorite song ready to listen to.

If you smoked marijuana, snorted cocaine, or used any drug or alcohol to enhance your mood, then you might need to find ways to improve your mood without relying on drugs.

If you used drug or alcohol to overcome your anger, then it's important to find healthier ways of dealing with anger.

G. Assign daily practice

Again, the mindfulness meditation audio recording is available to help you practice at home. Practice a formal mindfulness meditation at least once at home this week. In addition, practice one of the informal mindfulness practices each day, for example when eating or walking. I'd also like you to try mindfulness practices to notice triggers—thoughts, feelings, people—and your early reactions so that you can respond, or try the stop light metaphor or riding the roller coaster.

Write in a diary about when you felt cravings, and please go over and complete handouts 20 and 21 so we can discuss that next week.

H. Closing

Lead the client in the Awareness of Breath exercise, then end with three loving-kindness phrases (and, if time allows, a poem or a quote). Ring the bells softly three times and thank the participant for attending the session.

Meeting 6: Common Styles of Thinking

This session is important for introducing the concept of automatic thoughts and how our thoughts can impact our actions and feelings. It introduces an awareness of common styles of thinking; the concept of stopping to notice these thought reactions, especially during stressful situations; and the understanding that one can reframe these thoughts when they are unhelpful for us (Burns, 1989). Sometimes these common styles of thinking can be triggers for PTSD symptoms or for drug and alcohol use.

Meeting Preparation

Clinician Practice Read and familiarize yourself with the guided Sitting Meditation with Awareness of Thoughts and Feelings. Practice this meditation prior to this session and in preparation for guiding the adolescent. Be aware of your own feelings and senses when in session.

Materials

- Flipchart and markers
- Copy of Weekly Rating Sheet (handout 6)
- Handouts 22–23
- Meditation bells
- Folder of poems and quotes

Meeting 6 Outline

A. Formal mindfulness practice (10 minutes)

B. One-word check-in (2 minutes)

C. Review previous week's and today's intentions (5 minutes)

D. Weekly ratings (5 minutes)

E. Common styles of thinking—introduction (15 minutes)

F. Connection between thought, feeling, and action (10 minutes)

G. Assign daily practice (5 minutes)

H. Closing (5 minutes)

Meeting 6 Detailed Guide

A. Formal mindfulness practice

Lead the adolescent in the Loving-Kindness Meditation below, beginning with the following explanation:

This practice trains us to eventually connect with the boundless love, kindness, wisdom, and joy that is always present in all of us. It might seem very "busy" at first. We are invited to think of positive qualities of the heart, such as kindness, compassion, generosity, forgiveness, and patience; to allow ourselves to feel these qualities; and then to extend these good wishes: first to ourselves, then to other people who are dear to us, next to neutral people or strangers (those we see at school or outside but do not know well)—and finally to a difficult person, an enemy, or someone who has hurt us or is creating stress in our lives.

You can do this practice either lying down or sitting up. If you lie down and begin to feel that you are falling asleep, you can sit up.

Exercise: Loving-Kindness Meditation

You can begin by congratulating yourself for opening up time to take care of yourself. Become aware of the senses in your body, maybe by doing a one-minute body scan, noticing the thoughts and emotions that are present.

Shift your awareness to feel the direct sensations of the breath in your body. Notice the rhythmic movement of the breath in your body, selecting one part of the body to focus your attention on. The belly tends to be the easiest place for most people to "feel" the breath.

Connect with your heart, and allow it to be filled with all that is good. Allow yourself to be bathed by kindness and compassion, feeling it in every pore and cell.

Then begin to slowly repeat phrases of loving-kindness, allowing the meaning and feeling of the phrases to be part of you. You can begin with phrases such as these:

1. May I be safe. May I be protected. May I be healthy. May I learn to accept myself. May I have peace of mind. *Repeat these sentences two or three times, slowly and mindfully.*

2. *Expand the circle to include someone dear in your life, picturing the person in your mind's eye as clearly as possible. Offer him or her the loving-kindness phrases:* May he or she be safe. May he or she be protected. May he or she be healthy. May he or she learn to accept him- or herself. May he or she have peace of mind. *Repeat these sentences two or three times, slowly and mindfully.*

3. *Expand it to a neutral person or a stranger while continuing to repeat the phrases.*

4. *Extend it to a difficult person, an enemy, or someone who is creating difficulties or has hurt you. Don't force yourself to do anything. Notice if resistance arises. It is more important to notice what is happening than to be able to accomplish this step. Sometimes it takes months and years to forgive, and we have to learn to be patient with ourselves.*

End the meditation by focusing awareness to the breath again, feeling the in-breath and out-breath for a few moments, allowing the breath to nurture and nourish you.

Use the following inquiry to process the meditation that just finished:

What did you notice?

Were there any discoveries, any challenges you experienced while you did the meditation? Any emotions? Any feelings? Any bodily sensations? Take a moment to go inward and note what you are feeling or thinking.

Spend sufficient time processing this meditation with the adolescent, and practice it again in other sessions. It is often hard for individuals—adults or adolescents—to offer compassion to themselves or others. This practice can be very helpful in reappraising oneself and others, and it can be very healing. However, the adolescent should not feel forced to forgive or reconcile with others when he or she does not desire to do so. (See also the Loving-Kindness and Forgiveness Meditation script in appendix A, which helps in guiding this practice.)

B. One-word check-in

Can you check in with one word that kind of describes what you are experiencing this moment?

C. Review previous week's and today's intentions

Review what you discussed the week before, including the formal and informal mindfulness practices, and ask if the adolescent has any questions about **handouts 20 and 21** on thoughts, triggers, and coping strategies related to substance use.

What happened at home this week? Were you able to practice as requested?

What were some of the triggers you noted? Were you able to note what you felt or thought during those experiences? What coping strategies were you able to use? How did you feel using that strategy? Anything you would try again or try differently?

Review today's intentions, written on the flipchart.

D. Weekly ratings

Let's take a minute, as usual, so you can tell me how you have been feeling lately. First, I'll just ask you a few questions about how you may have been feeling. This will help us to understand how things are going and how we should move forward.

Refer to part A of **handout 6: Weekly Rating Sheet**—also found in appendix B—and proceed through the ratings and questions with the client. Afterwards, ask the client to review and think about part B of handout 6 prior to the next session.

E. Common styles of thinking—introduction and discussion

Today we are going to explore how upsetting feelings are usually linked to what you think and believe. What you think makes a big difference in how you feel. And, how you feel about any situation will depend on what you think about that situation.

"Common styles of thinking" are ways of thinking people sometimes use when they react to everyday events. These thinking patterns may be unhelpful, are not always true, and can lead to upsetting feelings. They are usually automatic; we don't even notice they are there. Learning how to identify, examine, and reframe thoughts that lead to unhelpful, upsetting feelings–which we call cognitive restructuring–is an important tool. We can be aware of what we are experiencing with kind curiosity, even with cravings or trauma-related feelings. It is helpful to be aware of what we are thinking or feeling and how we are acting or reacting at any moment.

Thoughts are not always true. Often we find that something that we held as absolutely true, when explored, is proven wrong. Also, thoughts are not permanent. Thoughts are actually like waves in the ocean that reach the shore, stay for a brief while, and then move away. Our task is not to chase after them or get engaged in the content of the thoughts. Instead, we are invited to allow thoughts in and let them flow out–like waves.

We are much larger than our thoughts. If we can observe or witness our thoughts and related emotions, bodily sensations, and perceptions, we learn that we are much larger than our thoughts and we can learn not to automatically react to them. This is a core mindfulness theme and the reason that practicing mindfulness can help us be aware of and respond to difficult situations.

Go over **handout 22: Common Styles of Thinking**—the contents of which are shown below—and try to elicit examples from the adolescent's own experiences. Identify situations when using drugs or alcohol might trigger trauma-related thoughts or, conversely, when PTSD-related thoughts might trigger drug or alcohol use. Does the adolescent use any of the common styles of thinking in these situations? What are some of them?

There are ways that we commonly think about things that can make us feel more sad, angry, or ashamed. Here are some of the common styles of thinking:

All-or-Nothing Thinking	The world is seen as totally bad or totally good with no shades of grey. Examples: *If I'm not perfect, I'm a failure.* *If I can't learn algebra in the next month, then I am a complete failure.*
Again-and-Again Thinking	You see a single bad event as a never-ending pattern. When something bad happens, you automatically assume that it will happen again and again. Examples: *Once a victim, always a victim.* *I was unable to keep myself safe before; therefore, I will always be unable to keep myself safe in the future.* *I will just keep getting hurt if I care about anyone—better to not care.*
"Must," "Should," or "Never" Thinking	These are unwritten rules or expectations for how you think you *should* behave that are based on myths, not facts. You may have learned these "rules" when you were really young and it may seem like they can never be changed. Yet, they may make you feel uncomfortable, anxious, afraid, sad, or angry. Examples: *I should be able to handle this.* *I never should have let it happen.* *I must stop thinking about my abuse.* *I should be able to do things all by myself.* *I should be [or should have been] stronger.*
End-of-the-World Thinking	These thoughts occur when you focus on the most extreme and distressing possible outcome. Many times they are triggered by "what if" thoughts or moments when, following a minor setback or unexpected problem, you find yourself assuming the very worst will happen. Examples: *I didn't do well on this exam. I'm going to flunk the class.* You lose your temper, yell at your family, and then think, *He (or she) hates me and will never want anything to do with me ever again.*

Thinking with Your Feelings	This is when what you feel determines what you think or believe. Sometimes feelings can be misleading. In fact, if you are anxious most of the time, your feelings are almost certainly lying to you sometimes. Examples: *I feel unsafe; therefore, I must be in danger.* *I feel ashamed; therefore, I must be a bad person.* *I feel sad, so my life must be hopeless.* *I feel angry, so somebody must be to blame.*
Too Much Risk	This occurs when you judge risk to be much greater than evidence would support. This way of thinking can lead to feeling lots of anxiety. It could help you feel better if you could better judge when there is danger and when there is not. Examples: *I'm not going to take a walk because I might be attacked.* Or, if you do live in a tough neighborhood, feeling that every place and neighborhood is too risky.
Always Blaming Yourself	This happens when you blame yourself for a bad outcome even if you had little or no part in causing it or you could not stop it. This way of thinking comes up when you take the blame yourself even when you have little or no responsibility. Examples: *It's my fault that this terribly sad event happened.* *My mother is upset, so I must be to blame.*
Thinking on the Downside	These thoughts occur when you selectively focus on a negative aspect of a situation or experience and ignore the positive. By focusing only on the negative, you do not see the "whole picture" and may feel worse than necessary. Examples: After a conversation in which you fumbled once for words, you say to yourself, *I'm such a screw-up, I made a total fool of myself.* *I had a lapse and I used drugs; I am a failure in everything I have tried up to now in recovery.*

Ask some of the following questions:

Which of these common styles of thinking have you experienced?

What are some of the situations that you have caused you to have these thoughts?

How did those thoughts make you feel?

What did you do when you felt that way?

The adolescent may have a hard time coming up with examples. Try to see if you can identify patterns from stories he or she has told you. Keep in mind that getting the exact names of the common styles right is less important than starting to note patterns in his or her life.

F. Connection between thoughts, feelings, and actions

Go over **handout 23: The Thoughts, Feelings, and Actions Triangle** to help introduce the most important concept: that thoughts, emotions, and responses (senses and actions) are interconnected and we can become aware of all three so as to make choices, that is, respond in a healthy way rather than react.

This diagram shows how our thoughts and feelings can interact, and how we can respond rather than react.

The Thoughts, Feelings, & Actions Triangle

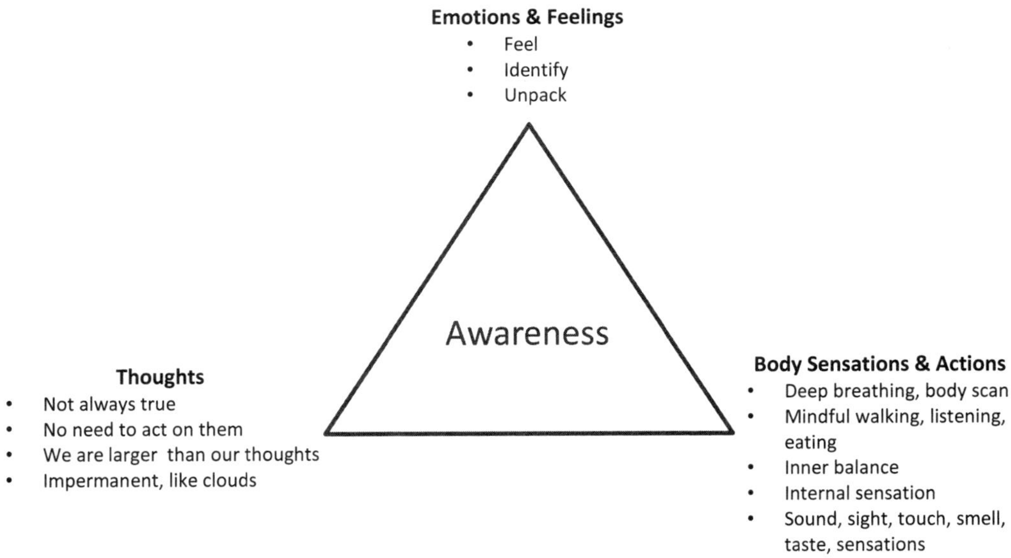

G. Assign daily practice

Again, the mindfulness meditation audio recording is available to help you practice at home. Practice a formal mindfulness meditation at least once this week. Also practice one of the informal mindfulness practices each day—for example while eating or walking. Try to identify the common styles of thinking that emerge in your daily life or in meditation. Use the STOP technique to notice how the thoughts make you feel and also how they come and go. What are some of the ways that you respond to those thoughts?

Assign the daily practice for the week and provide **handouts 22 and 23** for review.

H. Closing

End with three loving-kindness phrases (and, if time allows, a poem or a quote). Ring the bells softly three times and thank the participant for attending the session.

Meeting 7: Cognitive Restructuring—Observing Our Thoughts

This session focuses on learning the five steps of CR, which will assist the adolescent in identifying feelings and thoughts in the context of everyday situations and exploring those thoughts with curiosity. What is the thought, how does it make us feel, and what seems true or not so true about that thought? Is there another way to see the situation or understand that thought? Can we reframe it, that is, can we expand our awareness to the possible truths? How do we feel when we reframe or expand our understanding of the situation? These are some of the core questions in the five steps of CR. Your role as the therapist is to help the adolescent practice CR in a supportive way, transmitting the idea that this is an extension of building and expanding our awareness and exploring what we are experiencing with kindness and compassion.

Meeting Preparation

Clinician Practice As a preparation for witnessing the adolescent without judgment and with compassion, practice the Three-Minute Awareness of Breath exercise to help moderate moments of low energy or anxiety and to focus your presence in the moment. Before you start the session, do your own brief body scan, note how you are feeling, and prepare to be fully present in the session.

Materials

- Flipchart and markers
- Copy of Weekly Rating Sheet (handout 6)
- Handouts 23–27
- Meditation bells
- Folder of poems and quotes

Meeting 7 Outline

A. Formal mindfulness practice (5–7 minutes)

B. One-word check-in (2 minutes)

C. Review previous week's and today's intentions (5 minutes)

D. Weekly ratings (5 minutes)

E. Learning to watch what you think (10 minutes)

F. The five steps of cognitive restructuring (20 minutes)

G. Assign daily practice (5 minutes)

H. Closing (2 minutes)

Meeting 7 Detailed Guide

A. Formal mindfulness practice

Before we begin, I'd like to take a few moments to practice mindfulness. I will use words to guide you through this exercise.

Sitting Meditation with Awareness of Thoughts and Feelings, included in appendix A, is suggested for this session, but choose any you would like or ask the adolescent to indicate a preference. Afterwards, process the meditation with inquiry:

Were there any discoveries, anything that you noticed, any challenges you experienced while you did the meditation today? Take a moment to go inward and note what you are feeling or thinking.

B. One-word check-in

Can you check in with one word that describes what you are experiencing this moment?

C. Review previous week's and today's intentions

Review what you discussed the week before, including the formal and informal mindfulness practices. Explore the adolescent's responses regarding common styles of thinking:

Were you able to identify any common styles of thinking in the past week? What was the situation in which you noted that thought? What did you feel? What were some of the challenges? What are some others ways to look at the issue? Is there a need for compassion or kindness with yourself in looking at this?

D. Weekly ratings

Let's take a minute as usual so you can tell me how you have been feeling lately. First, I'll just ask you a few questions about how you may have been feeling. This will help us to understand how things are going and how we should move forward.

Refer to part A of **handout 6: Weekly Rating Sheet**, also found in appendix B, and proceed through the ratings and questions with the client. Continue with the following additional questions:

Now that we looked at how you've been feeling compared to a week ago, let's take a moment for you to tell me how you are feeling compared to a month ago.

On the 10-point scale where 1 is worst ever and 10 means no longer a concern, how would you rate your alcohol or drug use a month ago and how would you rate it now?

_______ RATING A MONTH AGO _______ RATING NOW

On the 10-point scale where 1 is worst ever and 10 means no longer a concern, how would you rate your PTSD symptoms a month ago and how would you rate them now?

_______ RATING A MONTH AGO _______ RATING NOW

On the 10-point scale where 1 is worst ever and 10 means no longer a concern, how would you rate your depressive symptoms a month ago and how would you rate them now?

_______ RATING A MONTH AGO _______ RATING NOW

On the 10-point scale where 1 is worst ever and 10 means no longer a concern, how would you rate your anxiety a month ago and how would you rate it now?

_______ RATING A MONTH AGO _______ RATING NOW

If there have been significant changes in any of the above symptoms, discuss the client's beliefs about what has led to the change(s). Afterwards, ask the client to review and think about part B of **handout 6** prior to the next session.

E. Learning to watch what you think

For many people, repeated negative thoughts, like blaming yourself or feeling sure that the worst will happen, are a big part of stress and depression. You can never say which part of the cycle comes first—whether negative thoughts cause depression or depression causes negative thoughts.

Today we'll work on learning how to notice your most common thoughts and to examine them. I am not expecting you to clear your mind of all or even any of your thoughts. Thoughts come and go. But I do want to help you notice them with curiosity. The first step is to pay attention to your thoughts and to notice how those thoughts can affect your mood, or how you feel. We have already started to do some of this in our previous meetings together. You have even started to practice doing this at home. Learning to "see" your own thoughts can help you to feel less controlled by them...your reactions to them are less automatic and you have the opportunity to respond.

We also have the opportunity to reframe, or see in a different way, what we are thinking or seeing. When we reframe a situation, we are trying to see if there are other ways to see this situation or thought.

Let's look at an example: Your friend is walking down the other side of the street. You say hello, but he or she doesn't respond. Your friend just walks by.

These could be your possible thoughts:

Thought 1: *He hates me.*

Thought 2: *I am a bad person.*

Thought 3: *My friend is a bad person; I hate him.*

Thought 4: *He didn't see me.*

Whenever we see something, our mind usually goes to our deeply ingrained ideas and patterned ways of seeing, and we miss seeing not only the whole picture but also the web of connections in which that situation is embedded. For example, in the example with your friend, what evidence do you have that your friend hates you or is a bad person?

What if you stopped to notice that your friend's mother was frantically calling him from up the street—what do you think then? What if you had missed that detail? What if we missed the idea that we were making some assumptions based on our beliefs about ourselves?

Differences Between Thoughts and Feelings

Remember previously we talked about common styles of thinking? Well those common styles of thinking tend to be very automatic. Before you know it, SNAP! They are there. It's useful to list a series of automatic thoughts so that we can see patterns in our thoughts.

We can also learn to notice the feelings associated with those thoughts. Before we begin, it's important to know the difference between thoughts and feelings. It's very common to think of the two as the same thing, but doing so makes it difficult to really get the most out of this list.

Thoughts are brief phrases of two or three words that we say to ourselves about ourselves, while a feeling is generally just one word. For example, you might say, "My school is too stressful." This is not a feeling but a thought about our school. The feelings that you might use in relation to this thought include stressed, anxious, sad, and bored.

Let's review ***handout 23: The Thoughts, Feelings, & Actions Triangle,*** *from last session. Note the differences between thoughts and feelings. How do thoughts seem different from feelings? How are they related to one another? You should feel free to return to this handout in your workbook, if you need help in remembering the difference between a thought and a feeling.*

Below the triangle are unhealthy thoughts, feelings, body sensations, and actions that people experience:

Thoughts

- *I am no good.*
- *It is my fault.*
- *Everyone is out to get me.*
- *There is always danger around.*

Emotions & Feelings

- Sadness and depression
- Guilt and shame
- Anger
- Fear and anxiety

Body Sensations

- Tension in the neck
- Tightness in the throat or stomach
- Pressure in the chest
- Numbness

Actions

- Using drugs and alcohol
- Fighting
- Doing things that are unsafe for me
- Carrying a weapon

F. The five steps of cognitive restructuring

A big part of the stress, anxiety, or depression we experience is related to the thoughts we have that make us feel bad, such as our worries or memories of the past. These thoughts are like colored glasses that cause us to see things around us in only one color, and don't let us see all the other colors that are present. That is, they do not allow us to see a situation clearly; everything gets painted the same shade.

Exploring the thoughts that make us feel bad, and being able to see a situation in a new way, can help us to change our feelings for the better. This is tough work, but you can do it. Our goal is not to get rid of all worries or negative thoughts. It is reasonable to worry about some things. That is normal and sometimes necessary. You just need to keep worry in its place.

There is strategy called "five steps" that I will teach you to help you understand, explore, and reframe the thoughts that make you feel bad. This strategy is like taking off a pair of sunglasses that only allows you to see one color so that you can see all the colors that are in front of you.

The technical term for this method is "cognitive restructuring." But you can think of it more simply as "expanding your thoughts." You will see as we work on this that when you reframe your thoughts or expand the possibilities, you can observe and transform the negative feelings that these thoughts create. It is not because your thoughts are "bad"; we all have all kinds of thoughts. But some thoughts are not as helpful to us. If we can observe our thoughts and our responses to them, then we can work with them. Sometimes it is helpful to see new options and possibilities.

Note to the clinician: Feel free to use any metaphor to explain CR.

First I'm going to show you the five steps by working through an example. Then we will try it with an example from your own life. [Have the adolescent look at **handout 24: The Five Steps of Cognitive Restructuring.**]

Exercise: The Five Steps of Cognitive Restructuring

These steps to cognitive restructuring are adapted with permission from Mueser, Rosenberg, and Rosenberg (2009).

Step 1: The Situation

In step 1, identify the situation and write it down on your handout. The situation could be something real, like needing to go to the store, having an argument with someone, or having a memory of a stressful event.

Step 2: The Feeling

Now in step 2, we want to identify the uncomfortable feeling related to the situation. It could be

fear
anxiety or stress
sadness or depression
guilt or shame
anger

Step 3: The Thought

In step 3, we want to identify your thoughts around the situation. Remember, thoughts usually lead to feelings, though sometimes we notice the feelings first. For example, we feel sad and then we notice we had a thought about missing our friend. Often we don't notice what we are thinking and we just move automatically to feeling sad, anxious, or angry. To work on this it will be helpful to identify as specific a thought as possible. Very general thoughts are more difficult to examine or reframe. Here are some examples of thoughts that can be reframed:

I am a bad person because I argued with my friend.
I will never be okay because of the abuse I had.
I will never make it to college because I flunked my exam.
I can't trust anyone because I will always be hurt by people.

Step 4: Examine Your Thought

In step 4, we want to create as much evidence as possible in favor of and against your thought. If it helps, make two columns, one for evidence for and one for evidence against. For example, for the thought I will never make it to college because I flunked my exam, *what evidence is there that you can make it to college? Have you passed other exams? What other things do you do well? Those go in the column for evidence against that thought. For the column for things supporting your thought, evidence may include that your grades are not good this year.*

Once you have generated evidence in favor of or against your thought, you are ready to decide whether the evidence supports or doesn't support your thought. Consider all the available evidence and decide if your thought or belief is correct or not. Ask yourself if you could convince another person that your thought is correct. Is there another way to see the situation?

If the evidence doesn't support your thought, create a new thought, a more accurate or useful one, to replace your old thought or at least to expand the possibilities. For example, I failed this exam but I have passed others; I still have a chance to go to college. I don't have to end here.

Step 5: Action Plan

If the evidence does support your thought, create a plan of action to help you respond to the situation, or to the effects of the automatic thought and your impulse to react. Is there something you can do to remind you of the other possibilities? How could your mindfulness practice help? Do you need support from a trusted friend? Is there a mantra you need to remember? Do you need added safety in the situation? Do you need to "ride the roller coaster"?

All are possibilities. What will work well for you? When can you do it? How?

Collaborate with the adolescent to select a situation that will prove useful for the CR exercise.

Let's practice the five steps together.

The problem you work with can be one identified during the weekly ratings. For example, if depression was most bothersome to the adolescent during the last week, concentrate on situations in which he or she might feel depressed. Be flexible. Using the selected situation, use **handout 24: The Five Steps of Cognitive Restructuring** to guide the adolescent through the steps.

G. Assign daily practice

This week, continue informal and formal practice of mindfulness. Go over the five steps of cognitive restructuring, and see if there is a situation you can explore using the five steps this week. Bring a situation for us to practice together using the five steps in our next session.

Assign the daily practice for the week and give the adolescent **handouts 23–27**, pertaining to the topics covered in today's session. Handout 25 is a portable card outlining the five steps; handout 26 explains in detail the categories of thoughts and feelings explored in CR; handout 27 puts the exercise in a convenient chart format. All of these can be helpful in the adolescent's practice of CR.

H. Closing

End with the full guided Loving-Kindness Meditation (see meeting 6) or three loving-kindness phrases (and, if time allows, a poem or a quote). Ring the meditation bells softly three times and thank the adolescent for attending the session.

Meetings 8–11: Mindfulness-Based CR and Recovery

The primary focus of meetings 8 and onward is the continued use of mindfulness and CR as well as practicing the recovery strategies on an ongoing basis.

In each session, use the different mindfulness exercises. Let the adolescent pick his or her preferred meditations or bring in appropriate poems, quotes, or song lyrics. There are abundant scripts in appendix A to guide you through meditations, but also feel free to be creative and to create meditations together as the adolescent's skills and practices develop.

The following table offers a general guide for what to include in these sessions:

Table 7.5 Intentions, Purposes, and Methods for Meetings 8–11

Intention	Purpose	Method
• Mindfulness practice and processing (10 minutes) • One-word check-in (2 minutes)	• Continue to build awareness and adolescent's mindfulness practice • Build capacity for responding mindfully on a daily basis	• Use scripts and create new practices together • Engage in informal and formal mindfulness practices

<table>
<tr><td>• Review content and assigned practice from last session (5 minutes)</td><td>• Solidify skills learned and encourage practice</td><td>• Ask questions about what the adolescent practiced at home and how that experience was
• Give feedback and answer questions to help refine skills</td></tr>
<tr><td>• Review intentions for today's session (2 minutes)</td><td>• Preview the intentions and tasks of the session</td><td>• Discuss goals and intentions</td></tr>
<tr><td>• Weekly ratings (5–10 minutes)</td><td>• Check progress and foster awareness of mood, anxiety, and substance use
• Explore situations or needs that the adolescent wishes to focus on (life situations, drug or alcohol use or related problems, mood)</td><td>• Use the Weekly Rating Sheet (10-point Likert scale format) to take the "temperature" of how things are going and progressing</td></tr>
<tr><td>Intention</td><td>Purpose</td><td>Method</td></tr>
<tr><td>• Core skill practice (CR, mindfulness for stress reduction) using current life situations and experiences whenever possible (30 minutes)
• Continue to plan for and evaluate readiness for change</td><td>• Encourage practices that will aid recovery from drug or alcohol use and improve functioning related to PTSD, trauma, and mood issues</td><td>• Use mindfulness practices
• Use CR with identified situations and thoughts
• Return to recovery skills regarding triggers, cravings, and motivations as needed
• Use Substance Use and Safety Plan and Measuring Change sheets as needed
• Conduct role-plays</td></tr>
<tr><td>• Assign daily practice
• Motivational reading and loving-kindness phrases (5 minutes)</td><td>• Encourage daily practice and integration of skills</td><td>• Assign practice to reinforce what was learned in the session
• Read poetry, quotes, or lyrics</td></tr>
</table>

In the final sessions, come to an agreement about the number of meetings remaining. You might taper meetings to every other week beginning sometime after meeting 10. Recall that at some point between meetings 8 and 10, it is helpful to have a conjoint parent-child session to review skills that the adolescent has learned and to enhance the likelihood of continued practice. It is important to elicit the adolescent's input regarding his or her progress and what you will focus on in the remaining sessions. Continue to use CR for examining ongoing situations and the adolescent's related thoughts, sensations, and feelings. Also use this opportunity to revisit any of the already developed skills and to review changes desired by the adolescent. Continue to invite the adolescent to bring in situations that can be used for role-plays, applied to CR, or considered for the development of an action plan or new coping strategy. And of course, continue to encourage mindfulness practices.

Meeting 12 (Or Final Meeting): Generalization Training and Termination

In the final session, it is important to review the progress made so far, and to create a self-care plan to ensure that the adolescent continues to make progress and maintain what he or she has learned. For some individuals, the symptoms of stress, depression, or anxiety may have almost disappeared. For others, they might still be present but can be better managed with the skills that have been learned. For still other adolescents, these symptoms might remain very strong. Whatever the case, the adolescent has learned many skills through this treatment that can continue to be of great value well into the future.

Meeting Preparation

Clinician Practice Take a few moments to connect with your breath, and do a two-minute body scan to inhabit the body more completely and to help yourself be more fully present for the adolescent in this, the final session.

Note to clinician: Prior to the session, consider inviting a parent or support person to attend so that he or she can gain an understanding of the skills the adolescent learned in treatment and encourage the adolescent to continue to use the skills. To prepare for this final session, create a certificate or some other way to commemorate the adolescent's significant accomplishment. Choose meaningful phrases that highlight your work with the adolescent and his or her investment in learning, practicing, and growing.

Materials

- Handout 28
- Meditation bells
- Folder of poems and quotes
- Certificate to commemorate the adolescent's accomplishment

Meeting 12 Outline

A. Process thoughts about treatment and termination

B. Review skills covered and progress made

C. Encourage practice

D. Referral for follow-up services (if needed)

E. Develop long-term plan

F. Closing: Commemorate the accomplishment

Meeting 12 Detailed Guide

A. Process thoughts about treatment and termination

Discuss with the adolescent his or her thoughts about the treatment and its ending: what he or she found helpful as well as any problems anticipated with using the skills independently after treatment ends. Help the adolescent begin to problem solve these concerns. If a parent or other support person is attending the session, consider facilitating the interpersonal dialogue practice presented in chapter 5, centered around appreciation for what has been accomplished as well as challenges and expectations. Questions that can be posed to the adolescent include, "What are you most appreciative of about doing this therapy?" and "What did you learn or gain?" Questions for parents include, "What have you noticed that has been learned, gained, or changed?" and "What have been the challenges?" And to both you might ask, "How might you help one another as you go forward?"

B. Review progress made and skills covered

Review the adolescent's progress and identify some plans that will help him or her to respond to difficult situations in the future.

Think about how you felt at the very beginning of treatment. What were you first feeling? How did your symptoms change during the course of treatment? Do you see any improvement? Are there any situations, thoughts, or feelings that are still difficult for you or that you think might be difficult for you in the future?

Remind the adolescent of the skills and information covered in the program, including the following:

- Mindfulness practice
- Education about PTSD and related symptoms
- Noticing and challenging common styles of thinking
- Being more aware of thoughts and feelings
- Communicating mindfully
- Responding mindfully to situations
- Making decisions about drug and alcohol use

C. Encourage practice

Emphasize the importance of practicing the skills learned. Use an analogy such as practicing a sport or a musical instrument.

You have to keep your skills up so you can apply them to the real game!

D. Referral for follow-up services

Identify any follow-up services, referrals, or activities that may be needed or beneficial. In particular, consider encouraging the adolescent to continue any other therapy he or she is involved in; to maintain involvement in, join, and/or obtain a sponsor for a twelve-step program (Narcotics Anonymous, Alcoholics Anonymous); to participate in an arts program; or to exercise. If it is an option, you can indicate that you can be contacted in the future if the adolescent needs or wants to return for further assistance.

E. Develop a long-term plan

Go over some of the questions and ideas on **handout 28: Summing Up.** Consider helping the adolescent record his or her responses to these questions to keep as a reminder and a written plan.

What things have gotten better since I started the program?

1.

2.

3.

What things do I still want to work on after the program ends?

1.

2.

3.

Which skills will help me to work on these things?

1.

2.

3.

What else do I need to be able to succeed in my goals?

1.

2.

3.

What can help me to remember to use my new skills in these situations, or whenever I am dealing with PTSD symptoms or my drug and alcohol use?

1.

2.

3.

F. Closing: Commemorate the accomplishment

Take time to give the adolescent feedback on his or her hard work and successes. Celebrate and commemorate the accomplishment by providing a certificate acknowledging the adolescent's ability to use all of the strategies and recognizing the skills gained (e.g., as a mindfulness practitioner, or as a master in riding the roller coaster of emotions). End with three loving-kindness phrases and, if you wish, a poem or a quote. Ring the bells softly three times and give thanks for the hard work you have done together.

Appendix A

Guided Mindfulness Scripts

Downloadable copies of this resource are available at http://www.newharbinger.com/31335. Please see the very back of this book for more details.

Sitting Meditation with Awareness of Sounds

Sitting in an erect and dignified posture; lowering the eyes or closing them; whatever is comfortable for you at this moment—allow your hands to rest on your legs or on your lap. Bringing your awareness to sounds. Notice sounds in this room, sounds outside the room, sounds near and far. Not making any efforts to listen to sounds, simply allow the sounds to come to you. This is pure hearing.

Noticing when the mind gets distracted with a story, planning, memories, thoughts of anticipation, regrets, blaming...and, gently and firmly, with kindness for yourself, redirect your mind to sounds. Notice if the mind has moved to judgments like *I like this sound* or *I don't like that sound*, and see if you can allow yourself to continue hearing regardless of your present likes or dislikes.

Bringing awareness to the silence between the sounds; just listening to whatever is coming to you in the form of sound.

And in the last few moments of this meditation, see if you can allow yourself to rest and nourish yourself by being right here, present to whatever is unfolding... accepting yourself exactly as you are and accepting everyone around you, including those difficult people in your life, exactly as they are...extending, with your thoughts, kindness and compassion to them.

And when you are ready, bring your attention back to the room, and allow your body to stretch—breathing deeply, releasing with the out-breath whatever you don't need right now, and with the in-breath, bringing new energy into your body.

[Bells]

Sitting Meditation with Awareness of Breath

Sitting in an erect and dignified posture: head, neck, and back straight, if that is possible for you; hands resting on your lap or on your legs, feet flat on the floor. Closing or lowering your eyes, whichever is most comfortable for you. Alert and relaxed, allowing your body to become still…fully present to yourself. Be aware of your thoughts: thoughts of anticipation, thoughts about feelings, thoughts about the past… Noticing your emotions, perhaps asking yourself: *How am I feeling right now? Am I peaceful, worried, frustrated…?*

And paying attention to your body, sort of "dropping" into your body for a few moments, and noticing how the body feels at this moment… Not wanting to fix or change anything. Choosing to respond instead of react to any impulses to stop, leave the room, or engage the attention of others. Allowing whatever you have noticed to move into the background…and now, placing your focus of attention on the direct sensations of the breath…

Not thinking about the breath, but feeling it. Feeling the direct sensation of the breath as it comes into the body and leaves the body. Without the need to change it, hold it, or control it. If you notice your mind attempting to shape the breath, or to control it, even in the smallest way, just noticing this tendency, and allowing the breath to flow freely.

Noticing that, with every inhalation, the abdomen and the chest expand, and with every exhalation the abdomen and the chest contract. Noticing the full cycle of the breath. You are not trying to do anything or to get anywhere.

And if your mind has wandered off the breath, notice where it went…and, without criticism, bring it back, gently and firmly, to this moment, to this breath. Be aware of any feelings and thoughts, and bring the mind back to the breath. If the mind leaves a hundred times in a few minutes, bring it back a hundred times, with kindness and lots of patience for yourself. Know that you and everyone else are all very imperfect beings, living in an imperfect world. That is okay.

In a few moments you will hear the bells. Allow the sounds of the bells to completely disappear before you move.

[Bells]

Sitting Meditation with Awareness of Thoughts and Feelings

Sitting in a dignified and erect posture: head, neck, and back aligned, if that is possible for you. Feet flat on the floor. Closing or lowering the eyes, whatever feels comfortable for you at this moment. Hands resting on your legs or on your lap, bringing your body to stillness.

And feeling the breath wherever it is most vivid in your body. You can choose to sustain your attention in the nostrils, noticing how the breath enters the nostrils, and perhaps perceiving the change in temperature when the breath enters and leaves the body. You can choose to feel the breath in the chest, noticing how the chest rises and falls with the breath. The easiest place for most people to feel the breath and to notice the rhythmic movement of the breath is in the belly, in the abdomen. If you like, bringing your attention to the belly right now...and noticing how the abdomen expands with the in-breath and deflates with the out-breath, allowing the breath to flow freely.

You may notice as you sit here, breathing, that there are thoughts present in your awareness.

Noticing thoughts is the focus of concentration now—observing the process of thinking itself. Allowing your thoughts to move to the foreground, taking center stage in your awareness... Noticing how the mind may want to follow the thoughts, and gets trapped in the content of the thoughts, wanting to expand upon them and construct stories. Whatever the content may be, whether the thoughts are about the past or the future, whether they are judgments, opinions, fantasies, dreams—just being aware of how the mind is attracted to or repelled by certain thoughts. Noticing how some thoughts are pursued by the mind and some are rejected... Then practice letting the thoughts be. Simply witnessing each thought, as it comes up in the mind, as an observable event—a unit in the field of awareness, with a beginning, a middle, and an end. Observing the coming and going... how thoughts arise, linger briefly or for an extended period, and then pass away...the thoughts fading and dissolving, "just like clouds."

If you find yourself being drawn into the current of thinking, realize that you are no longer observing the thoughts but that you are lost inside them...and when you become aware of this, just coming back to the observation of thoughts as separate elements…as clouds in the sky, drifting through the spacious vast sky of the mind.

Sometimes the thoughts may become disturbing, too charged for you to simply observe them. If this happens, know that it is always possible to return to the breath. Use the breath to anchor you, to stabilize you in the present moment.

You may notice that there are also emotions that are arising in the body and in the mind. Allowing yourself to feel any emotion that is present at this moment with the intention to make room for whatever is arising moment-to-moment. Maybe there is a feeling of boredom, impatience, or restlessness. You may be experiencing peaceful feelings, like contentment, happiness, or joy…or less peaceful ones, like sadness, anxiety, or frustration, anger, or fear. Being aware of what you are experiencing as emotions, in this moment.

Observing how some emotional states, like happiness and contentment, are welcomed or held on to, or how you may be running away from or blocking or fighting emotions like anxiety, fear, anger, or sadness. Observing whatever emotion is present with a sense of exploration and welcoming the emotion, if that is possible for you. Allowing whatever emotions are present to come and go without "doing" anything about them… Noticing how they arise, how they occupy the mind for a while and then fade away…

Knowing that if, at any time, emotions or feelings become too strong or too intense, it is always possible to return to paying attention to the feeling of breathing, feeling the breath as it enters the body and leaves the body…

And now allowing, if you like, the breath to nourish you and nurture you for a few moments… Knowing that the breath could become your home base and your ally to help you navigate moments of distress or difficulty, and to help bring you back to your balance at any moment… And allowing the benefits of this practice to flow into the entire experience of your life…

[Bells]

Loving-Kindness and Forgiveness Meditation

Sitting or lying down, whatever is most comfortable for you at this moment. Being aware of the breath and sensations throughout the body. Being fully present to the sensations of contact with the chair or floor, feeling its support. Noticing the rhythmic movement of the breath, coming and passing away... And as you're sitting or lying down, allowing the region of the chest to become the primary focus of attention. Noticing if the middle of the chest feels tight and contracted, or if it feels warm, open, and expansive... There is no need to change anything. If it's possible, bringing an accepting, open, and accommodating awareness to whatever is present in the middle of the chest...

Being attentive as well to the underlying vastness inside you, present at all times, in all of us. Notice what is "underneath"—connecting to the center of your being.

And, remembering the ways in which you have harmed yourself by judging yourself harshly and lacking kindness for yourself...with the intention to forgive yourself, knowing that at this moment, you can start a fresh new life. Knowing also that we don't forgive for the sake of others; we forgive for our own sake, so we can have more freedom and peace in our lives...

The term *loving-kindness* encompasses the qualities of *benevolence*, *patience*, *compassion*, *gentleness*, *forgiveness*, and *unconditional love*. Seeing if you can connect with any of these qualities, even only some... You may choose to continue paying attention to the breath or sounds, and that is perfectly fine. Also, if at any point you feel anxious, frightened, or restless, know that at any point you can always go back to paying attention to the breath or sounds.

And if you like, connecting to that boundless source of peace, kindness, and forgiveness already inside of you... Seeing if you can allow yourself to be bathed in this positive and nourishing energy... And if you like, use any phrases that you find appropriate to shower yourself with love and kindness. You could use the following sentences:

May I learn to forgive and accept myself.

May I be safe and protected from inner and outer harm.

May I be as healthy and strong as is possible for me.

May I learn to care for myself with joy and ease.

And having established this radiant center of love and kindness, if you like, you could think of someone who is dear to you, even if that person is no longer alive: a parent, a sister, a brother, a teacher, or a friend. And holding that person in *your mind's eye and in your heart*, wish that person *happiness*. Asking that person for forgiveness for the suffering that you may have caused.

And if you like, saying to that person:

I forgive myself and ask for your forgiveness.

And if you find that you are having a difficult time forgiving yourself, being with that part that is resisting forgiveness and extending love and compassion to your loved one and to yourself, say:

May you be happy.

May you be free of suffering.

May you be peaceful.

And use any other wishes that you would like to give to that dear person in your life.

And return to the breath, allowing the breath to flow freely, nourishing yourself with the breath. And, when you are ready, bringing to your mind's eye and your heart all the people that you love dearly, and sending them boundless loving-kindness...

And now, continue to experience loving-kindness, bringing to your mind's eye and your heart a neutral person, a person you have *no relationship with*. Someone you see sometimes—a shopkeeper, someone you see often in hallways, and sending kind thoughts to that person.

And if you like, saying to that person:

May you be happy.

May you be free from suffering.

May you be peaceful.

And if you like, ask for forgiveness for all those times when you were unkind to strangers or people you did not know very well.

And now, think of all the strangers who have been extremely kind and helpful to you, and send them boundless loving-kindness.

And thinking now of someone *whom you have had difficulties with*, someone who has been or is right now challenging in your life. Notice what arises just by thinking of that person, what happens in your body, what your thoughts are…and notice any feelings and emotions that arise. There is no need to "force" yourself to be kind and compassionate to that person. Forgiveness is a process. Be gentle and kind with yourself.

Only if you feel that you have the resources to extend kindness, you may want to say to that person:

May you be happy.

May you be free from suffering.

May you be peaceful.

And now, see if it is possible to send kindness and compassion to all beings in the entire world…

May all be happy.

May all be free from suffering.

May all be peaceful.

And going back to the breath for a few moments before we end this meditation. Allowing the breath to replenish you and ground you in the present moment.

[Bells]

Seated Body Scan

Sitting with your eyes open and lowered, or choosing to close your eyes if that is more comfortable for you right now. Bringing your attention to your breath, feeling the direct sensations of the breath, the movement of the breath, wherever the breath is most vivid for you at this moment. You might feel the breath in the nostrils, or in the chest... Notice how the chest rises with the in-breath and contracts with the out-breath... Or you might feel the breath in the abdomen or your belly... Notice how it rises with the inhalation and deflates with the exhalation... And with each exhalation softening the body and allowing the body to rest deeper into the support provided by the chair. If you like, you can place your hands on the abdomen or your belly for a few moments to feel the rhythmic movement of the breath.

And now, expanding your attention to your whole body, notice how your body feels at this moment. Is there any tension in the body, any tiredness? Allowing yourself to feel any emotion or sensation, making room for whatever you are feeling at this moment; not wanting anything to happen, not even relaxation.

Bring the mind back to the body with gentleness and firmness whenever you notice that it has wandered off.

And notice the contact that the feet are making with the floor. Do you feel the support of the floor, or any sensations in your feet right now? Silently noting what you are feeling... Notice any sensations in your feet. Are you feeling sensations of warmth or coolness, tingling, throbbing in your feet? Do you notice the contact that the feet are making with the floor? Can you detect any other sensations in your feet?... Maybe you are not aware of any sensations, and that is totally fine. Just noticing that you are not feeling anything is what's important... Move your attention up through the legs. Do you feel the contact of your sitting bones with the chair? Are you experiencing a sense of warmth, pulsing, pressure, tingling, or anything else? It's totally fine if you don't feel anything. Just notice if you feel or don't feel sensations...

And when you are ready, move your awareness to the back, the lower back. We tend to accumulate a lot of tension in the lower back. Notice if there is discomfort in the lower back at this moment. If you like, exhale, imagining that the discomfort leaves with the out-breath, and that with the in-breath you are bringing freshness and new energy to the body... Aware of sensations in the middle back, notice the movement of the rib cage with the breath. Pay attention to sensations in the shoulder blades, the upper back—notice how the shoulders feel. Expand your awareness to explore sensations in your entire back...

If your attention has wandered away or has been hijacked by a story, planning, regrets, memories, and so on—which happens to all of us whenever we practice focusing on something—realize where your mind went and gently, firmly, and with curiosity, with a lot of kindness and patience for yourself, and without criticizing or blaming yourself, escort your attention back to exploring sensations in the shoulder area…

And now notice sensations on the sides of the body. Maybe become aware of the movement of the rib cage. And when you are ready, bring your attention to the front of the torso, and become aware of the physical sensations in the pelvic area. Move your awareness up to your abdomen… Perhaps you will notice how the abdomen and belly contract and expand with the breath. Notice sensations in the stomach, maybe sensations related to digestion…

Move attention up to the chest. Does the middle of the chest feel expanded or contracted? No need to do anything, just notice. Notice any sensations in the area around the heart, perhaps detecting the beating of the heart at this moment… And move your awareness down through the arms to the hands and fingers. Notice if the fingers are tense, and whether any other sensations are present in the fingers: any sweat, tingling, throbbing? Be aware of the sensations in the palms; are the palms hot or cold? What are you experiencing deep inside the hands? Feel the changing sensations in your arms, the skin, and the touch of the clothes that you are wearing, the muscles and bones. Just notice anything that is present, being with what is present right here, right now.

And now, allowing your attention to move to the shoulders and to the back of the neck and the throat area. Becoming aware of sensations in the back of the head, in the scalp area, the skull, the top of the head, deep inside the head; sensations in the forehead…the ears…deep inside the ears and the outside of the ears… the area around the eyes…the eyes…eyebrows…eyelashes…the nose and nostrils… the lips and inside the mouth…the cheeks and jaw area… Aware of sensations in the whole face, notice if you are holding tension in the face.

And when you are ready, hold the entire body in your awareness, from the top of the head to your feet. Be aware of the breath flowing freely in and out of the body. Know that at any moment during the day or night you can experience a relaxed and awake state by connecting with the direct sensations of your breath in your body. Allowing yourself to feel that rhythmic movement of the breath…

And when you are ready, opening the eyes if they were closed, and bring awareness to the room where you are, stretching for a few moments if you need to stretch.

[Bells]

Seated Body Scan Interspersed with Mindful Movement

While doing this exercise it is important to be gentle with yourself. If you try too hard to be relaxed, you can create discomfort in your body, and in your mind. Simply observe what is happening, with a sense of exploration and curiosity. Remembering that there is no right way to feel… Giving yourself permission to feel what you're feeling… Notice the desire to judge your feelings, to want things to be different than they are right now. Just allowing yourself to be exactly the way you are…

We are going to do this body scan from a sitting posture interspersed with movement. And so now, sitting in a comfortable chair, feet flat on the floor, hands resting on your knees or thighs… The eyelids lowered, or closed, whatever you prefer. In a relaxed and aware position, bring awareness to your breath. Feeling the direct sensations of your breath, with no need to modify it or change it in any way… Maybe you'd like to place your hands on your abdomen for a few moments… Notice the abdomen rising with the in-breath, and falling or contracting with the out-breath. Just follow this for a few moments, getting a sense of this rhythmic movement…

If you like, you can imagine bringing new energy, freshness, and vitality into your body when you breathe in; and cleansing, releasing toxins, every time you breathe out. With the body scan we are training our minds to be in the present, to live in the "here and now." So, whenever you notice that your mind has wandered away from the breath or the scanning, bring it back gently and firmly, with no judgment. Being very kind and gentle with yourself…

Also remember that if, at any moment, you feel a lot of anxiety due to body memories, flashbacks, or any other negativity or discomfort experienced either in your body or in your mind, you can always use the breath or sounds as a place of refuge to bring you back to your center, to yourself, to the present moment.

And now, if you like, removing your hands from the abdomen and placing them again on your thighs or knees…

And now, moving your awareness from the abdomen all the way down, through the legs, down the legs, until you reach your feet… If you like, you can move the toes however you want to move them, exploring with great curiosity the sensations present in your toes… Perhaps you may notice warmth or coolness, moisture or dryness, a tingling sensation… And now penetrating with your attention inside the feet… Just notice what is present. You may not feel anything, and that is perfectly fine.

And now, bringing awareness to the rest of the legs. Scanning for sensations in your legs. Perhaps noticing the contact that the legs are making with the chair. Aware of bones, ligaments; aware of any uncomfortable, even painful, sensations… If you like, using the breath to soften and open to all that is present, with the intention of accepting things exactly as they are and accepting yourself exactly as you are.

And now, let's do some movements for the legs and feet. Lifting the right first, flexing the right foot up and down, circling the right foot to the right, and to the left; moving your toes; placing your right leg down. And now, lifting the left leg, flexing the left foot, circling the left foot first to the left and then to the right; moving your toes; aware of sensations. Placing your left leg down.

When you are ready, bringing awareness to the torso. Moving awareness to the pelvic area, aware of any sensations present in this area. And paying attention to sensations in the lower back… We tend to accumulate a lot of tension in the lower back. If you are noticing that there is discomfort in the lower back, you can choose to imagine that you are allowing this area to fill with freshness and energy while you breathe in and when you breathe out, imagining that all the tension, discomfort, pain leaves the body with the out-breath. Aware now of sensations in the midback, perhaps noticing the rib cage moving with the breath… Paying attention to sensations in the upper back, the shoulder area. If you like, releasing and softening any tension that you notice with the out-breath, and bringing new life and freshness with the in-breath… And now, let's do some movement for the shoulders. On an in-breath, bringing the shoulders close to your ears, and dropping them on the out-breath. Rotate your shoulders backwards. Rotate your shoulders forward. Aware of all sensations.

And now, moving your awareness to the front of the torso, carefully exploring any sensations in the abdomen. Maybe notice the abdomen rising when you breathe in, and deflating when you breathe out… Paying attention to sensations in your belly. Maybe aware of digestion. Allowing things to be just the way they are right now… And moving awareness up through the body to the chest. Does the chest feel contracted or expanded right now? No need to do or change anything. Just notice…

And moving attention down through the arms to the hands and fingers. Aware of any sensations present in your fingers, in the palm and top of your hands, the wrists, the lower arms, the elbows, upper arms, and shoulders. Totally aware of all sensations present in these parts of your body… And when you are ready, lifting both arms in front of you, and circling the hands to the right, and to the left. Flexing your hands up and down. Opening and closing the hands while you spread the fingers wide, feeling all sensations. Aware of the in-breath and out-breath.

And moving your awareness up to your head and neck. Detecting sensations in the back of the neck and the throat area… Just notice whatever is present. No need to "do" anything or change, suppress, or try to "conquer" any feeling or thought that may be present. Paying attention to sensations in the back of the head, deep inside the head, and the top of the head… Moving attention to the face, experiencing the entire face… Scanning for sensations, paying attention to your breath. Allowing your face to relax…

And now experiencing the entire body, aware of non-doing; just existing in this quiet, in this silence and stillness, letting the breath flow freely and easily. Feeling complete, with the ability to tap into your immense inner resources. Experiencing your capacity to be connected to the world…

And return to an awareness of the place where you are right now—maybe opening your eyes, if you had them closed…and moving in whatever way feels right to you, allowing the calmness and the centeredness that you may be feeling right now to remain with you.

[Bells]

Walking Meditation

Standing in the mountain pose*, aware of your breathing, bring your awareness to the soles of your feet. Notice the support and connection with the floor at this moment. Shift the weight of the body to the right leg and, on an inhalation, lift the left foot...and, exhaling, place it in front of you, heel first. And shift the weight of the body to the left leg, and inhaling, lifting the right foot...and exhaling, placing it in front, heel first. And continue to do this, inhaling—lifting; exhaling—placing.

Next expand your awareness to include sensations in the legs for a few moments, and lastly, expand the field of awareness even wider to include the whole body. Notice sensations in your entire body with every step. And if you notice that your mind has been caught in a story, that it is in a blaming, judging mode, notice that, and gently direct your attention back to feeling sensations of movement in your entire body...

Now coming to an ending... Lower your eyes and notice how your body feels. What are the thoughts and emotions present at this moment?

[Bells]

* If you are unfamiliar with this pose, see "Mindful Standing Stretching Practice," later in this section.

Eating Meditation (with Raisin)

Pretend that you have just arrived from another planet and that you have to report what you just received. You have never seen these objects before. So, taking one of these objects in your hand, observe it with curiosity. Please tell me what you see—color, shape, texture, size… Now hold it between your fingers, and see what you notice (*it's sticky, rough*; *has edges*, *is malleable*, and so on). With exquisite attention, bring the object to your nose and tell me what you notice now… Now bring the object to your ear and move it around close to the ear. Is there anything that you can hear?… Dispose of that object.

Now, with great awareness to how your arm and hand move, bring another object to your lips. Notice sensations on the lips, the air touching the object, and anything else that you can detect. Place the object in your mouth, but don't bite it. Notice if there is an impulse to swallow. Just move it around in your mouth… What are you noticing now? And, when you are ready, begin to chew the object. Chew, and chew, and chew. Notice if you are in a hurry. Just notice whatever comes up in relation to this tiny object… If your attention wandered away from the sensations of chewing, notice that, and bring your attention back to what you are doing. Concentrate… Chew slowly, carefully, paying total attention to what you are doing… If you notice that your mind goes into a thought, a story, a like or dislike, notice that and bring the mind back to what you are doing—chewing. Chew and pay attention with full awareness… And when you are ready, swallow the object with full attention to all the sensations present. Bring your awareness to the breath for a few moments; notice the breath coming into the body and moving out of the body.

[Bells]

Riding the Roller Coaster of Emotions Meditation

This meditation is adapted with permission from the "Urge Surfing" exercise in Bowen, Chawla, and Marlatt (2011).

Often times our emotions and lives can be like riding a roller coaster. One moment we are happy; the next moment we are feeling angry or anxious about something, triggered by the things that are happening around us. Have you ever been on a roller coaster ride? A roller coaster is a fast-paced ride, with slow moments as the car rides up an incline with us inside, waiting in anticipation for the next fall. There can be a euphoria (an emotional high) as the car falls forward down the roller coaster track, but there can be fear there, too. Our emotions can run like a roller coaster too; even if we are not aware, we are pulled into the feelings and reactions of those twists and turns, rising and dips. What if you could learn to be aware of those turns, slow things down a bit when you want to and ride the roller coaster with attention and responsiveness?

You can do this meditation when you are feeling out of center, reactive, euphoric, in danger of relapsing, or simply to get to know your emotions more intimately. If you have the opportunity and space, before you begin this meditation it might help to do some slow mindful stretches, or walking meditation.

In order to begin this meditation—**Pause**, or **Stop**—disconnect from whatever you are doing. At times, due to the circumstances at that moment, it might be hard to physically stop. Regardless of whether you can stop externally, in order to do this mindfulness meditation, it is important that you stop internally, with the intention to pay attention, with affectionate curiosity, to whatever is arising in your body and mind at that moment. Start by silently saying a few loving-kindness phrases such as, *May I accept myself exactly as I am in this moment and make room for whatever is arising in this moment. May I learn to be kind and compassionate to myself. May I be peaceful, clear, and well.*

Begin by sitting comfortably or lying down, with your eyes closed or open. **Bring your attention to sounds or the feeling of the breath** in your body wherever you feel the breath most vividly. If you choose to pay attention to sounds, just allow sounds near and far to come to you, without making any effort. If you choose to pay attention to the breath, there is no need to manipulate the breath, allow the breath to flow freely and normally. If the breath is shallow and burdened, allow it to be that way; if it is long and deep, just notice that it is that way.

In paying attention to the breath, you may choose to place one hand on your belly and another hand on your chest, allowing yourself to feel the expansion of the belly and the chest with the inhalation, and the flattening or deflation with the exhalation. If you find that your mind is very agitated, you can label the movement. Inhaling—*rising, expanding.* Exhaling—*falling, contracting.* Choose a word that is easy for you to label the movement of the breath.

Formulate the intention to remain free of judgment and be openhearted throughout the meditation, allowing kindness and compassion for yourself to be present. It might happen that you begin to feel a slight kindness for yourself or not. It is possible that you continue to feel defective and unworthy. It does not matter whether the feeling is pleasant, unpleasant, or neutral. Noticing the way you feel and allowing yourself to feel the way that you are feeling is what matters. Note that it takes courage and determination to do this work.

After feeling the direct sensations of sound or the breath for a few minutes, **bring your attention to the sensations present in your body:** discomfort, pain, heaviness, contraction, hot or cold in the extremities or the face, dry mouth, sinking feeling in the pit of the stomach, a lump in the throat, or anything else that is present. Do a one-minute scanning of your body, moving your fingers or toes, legs and shoulders if necessary to heightened sensation. Go back to paying attention to the breath whenever you feel a strong urge, a craving, or an impulse to act in a destructive way to yourself or to another. Ride the roller coaster of sensations using the breath as an anchor to help you be with the reactivity and the desire to "do" something. Choose "non-doing." Put the brake on instead of pressing the accelerator.

Shift your attention to notice any feelings or emotions that might be present, with the intention to befriend and make room for all emotions. Notice clearly the feelings and emotions that are present: where do you feel them in your body? What is their texture, color, taste, or smell? There might be feelings of sadness, euphoria, happiness, shame, fear, confusion, or anger. There is usually more than one feeling or emotion present. See if it is possible for you to select one emotion as the object of your exploration, with the intention to perceive, as clearly as possible, the signature of that feeling or emotion in your body. Are there any changes in the emotion? How? What is your relationship to that emotion: are you pushing it away or are you noticing attachment to it? Notice that in the middle of an unpleasant or disturbing emotion might be a pleasant feeling and vice versa. If it becomes too difficult and overwhelming, choose to go back to the refuge of resting with the awareness of sounds or the breath.

Shift your attention to the thoughts that are present in your mind. There may be thoughts of anticipation, memories, stories about similar situations. Allow the thoughts to flow in and out of your mind, being careful not to get entangled in the content of the thought. Become aware that if you can witness your thoughts, you are much larger than your thoughts. Realize that your thoughts are events in the field of your awareness; that, like emotions and bodily sensations, they arise, stay for a while, and quickly disappear if you don't do anything to hold them. Go back to the awareness of sounds or the breath every time that you feel out of balance or disturbed.

Finish the exercise by **narrowing your awareness to the feeling of the breath** in your body: paying attention to the entire duration of the in-breath, the entire duration of the out-breath, and perhaps noticing the gap in between the in-breath and the out-breath. Allow the breath to nourish you for a few moments before you end the meditation.

[Bells]

Mindful Standing Stretching Practice

Let's begin this mindful stretching practice with some standing postures. Allow yourself to explore with curiosity and without judgment all the sensations that arise moment-to-moment. Remember throughout to coordinate breath and movement and to let this practice be a time of mindful care for you.

Mountain: So now, let's begin by standing with your feet directly under your hips, feeling as much of the soles of the feet as possible...aware of your toes, the heels and the solid support of the floor. And moving awareness up through the body, bringing a gentle lift through the arches, the ankles, and the lower legs, knees, upper legs, and up through the spine, shoulders at ease, the chest is open...head, neck, and back aligned, if that is possible for you...the head balanced on the neck and shoulders, arms alongside the body... Experiencing a sense of presence and elevation just like a mountain.

Arm Stretch: Lift the arms toward the ceiling and stretch, as if trying to touch the ceiling. Feeling the sensations present in your body, the sides of the body, in the arms, hands and fingers, in the lower back, and legs. And with the left hand holding the right wrist, stretch the right arm as much as possible...feel the sensations in the arm and the right side of the body. And with the right hand, hold the left wrist, and stretch the left arm... Notice all that is happening, aware of the breath. And on an exhalation, allow the arms to float down.

Horizontal Arm Stretch: Now, inhaling and allowing the arms to flow up to shoulder level, elbows straight, flexing your wrists so that your palms face the sides of the room. Aware of the air and sensations in the arms, the wrists, the armpits, and all the muscles that are engaged. Exhaling, and slowly and mindfully, allowing the arms to flow down.

Picking Grapes: And now we will do what we call picking grapes. Taking a deep breath in...and lift just the right arm. Stretch, feeling the stretch all along the right side of the body, the rib cage, the arm and the hand. Stretch, and reach toward the ceiling, in the direction of something that you really want, some juicy grapes that are just out of your reach.

Continue to let the breath flow freely, and if you like, increase the stretch by lifting up the left heel, at the same time, reaching, stretching... Lower the left heel, and slowly let the right arm float back down to the side. Stand once again in the mountain pose. Notice how the right arm and the right part of the body feels. Notice how the left side feels. Inhale, lifting the left arm, stretching, reaching toward those grapes that are just out of reach; and if you wish, let the right heel come up, increasing the stretch… Exhale and lower the right heel and allow the arm to flow down to the side of the body.

And standing once again in the mountain pose, fully present, experiencing whatever physical sensations come into your awareness. Be aware of your breathing, the breath flowing in and out of the body.

Crescent Moon: Inhaling and bringing the arms up overhead, pressing the palms together. Exhaling and bending to the left and allowing the hips to move to the right, exploring if you can continue to extend through your fingers. Allowing the breath to flow freely, noticing the quality of the breath, where you feel it most vividly, and aware of the sensations on the right side of your body. Inhaling, bringing the arms back to center. Stretching up, trying to touch the ceiling, feeling the stretch throughout your body. Inhaling and on the exhale, bending to the right and allowing your hips to move to the left. Aware of sensations on the left side of your body and anything else that is here right now. Noticing any thoughts, emotions, your mood. Feeling this stretch through the elbows and the armpits… through the rib cage…right out of the pelvis, and anywhere else that you feel it along your body… from head to toe. And inhaling and on the exhale bringing the body and arms back to center. Closing the eyes, aware of the rhythmic movement of the breath, moving in and out of the body.

Shoulder Rolls: And now we are going to do some shoulder rolls. Inhaling, bringing the shoulders up to the ears, holding the breath, and exhaling through the mouth, allowing the arms to drop down. Then rolling the shoulders back—aware of the shoulder blades, squeezing toward each other, and the chest expanding—and letting the shoulders drop down. And rolling forward, squeezing the shoulders toward each other, and continuing to roll through these four places, up and back, down and forward, in your own time. And when you're ready, roll back in the opposite direction, up and forward, down and back…

Bringing the body to stillness, standing, feeling the effects of what we just have done…feeling all the sensations present in the neck and shoulder region.

Neck Stretch: And now we will do some stretches for the neck. Inhale and exhale, allowing the right ear to move toward the right shoulder, keeping the right shoulder relaxed. Aware of any sensations present in the left side of the neck, breathing into the tender places… And inhaling, bring the head back to center. Repeat on the other side. And when you are ready, inhale and exhale, bringing the chin to the chest, aware of sensations in the throat and back of the neck. Inhale and look up, keeping the back of the neck long. Bring the head back to center. Return to mountain. Let the body be completely relaxed, but at the same time alert, poised, balanced, as you continue to be aware of your breathing.

Tree: And now let's do the tree…from the mountain pose, allowing the entire weight of your body to shift to the right leg and placing the sole of your left foot into the right inner thigh, lower leg, or even allowing the toes to touch the floor, careful not to place your foot directly on the knee. Place the palms together in the middle of the chest in a clapping posture. And picking out a spot either on the wall, or on the floor three or four feet in front of you, focus your gaze on that spot.

And when you're ready, inhaling and stretching the arms up over your head as far as they'll go. And clasping your fingers together—pressing the upper arms against your ears. And breathing deeply down into your abdomen. And just balancing here, if possible keeping the left knee straight.

When you're ready, inhaling and on the exhalation slowly unclasping your hands and letting the arms come down to the side. And when they are about horizontal, lifting the knee up, and bringing the right foot down alongside the left foot. And taking a deep breath in and out here. And then allowing the weight to shift to the left leg as you shift the right foot and place it inside the left leg…wherever it will go… Place the palms together in the middle of the chest in a clapping posture. And when you feel balanced, inhaling and stretching your arms up over the head, and clasping the hands again. Pressing the upper arms against your ears as you breathe and balance. Stretching a little bit higher… And then unclasping the hands, and slowly letting the arms come down until they're horizontal…when you'll lift the right knee up and slowly come down with the arms and the foot… And then you're standing again on both feet. Allowing your eyes to close… And centering your awareness in your abdomen…and your body as a whole, as you stand here allowing the breath to flow freely.

Balancing Pose: And now we will do a balancing pose. Begin by centering yourself in the mountain pose. Focus the eyes on a place on the floor three to four feet in front of you. Slowly, let the weight shift over onto the left leg, and then extend the arms to the sides so that they are parallel to the floor, and on an inhalation lift the right leg to the side, and balance on the left foot, breathing. Your left leg is firmly planted, rooted, and you are maintaining your balance as best as you can. Be sure you are breathing. The breath continues to flow freely…

And when you are ready, slowly let the leg and arms come down. You are standing once again in the mountain pose…

On an inhalation, lift the arms and extend them to the side, gazing three to four feet in front of you. And when feeling balanced, lift the left leg, aware of what you have to do to maintain the balance. Breathe and be aware of sensations. Exhale and bringing the arms down, the leg down, and back into the mountain pose, aware of sensations throughout the body, aware of your breath.

Standing Twist: And now placing your hands on your hips, inhale and exhaling, turn the head as far to the right as possible, maintaining the shoulders where they are. Seeing if you can look behind as you turn your head to the right. Feeling the stretch in this position, breathing into it. And on an inhale allowing the head to come back to center. Repeat on the other side. And now, inhaling and exhaling while gently twisting and turning from the waist, allowing the head and neck to follow. The hips are facing forward, only the head and the upper torso are turning. Inhaling and coming back to center. Repeat on the other side.

And now, keeping your hands on your hips, inhale and exhaling, turning from the ankles so that you are turning your whole body as far as you can to the right, except the feet. Tracking with the eyes, going as far as you can to the right, breathing, stretching. Inhaling and coming back to center. Repeat on the other side. Return to mountain.

Forward Bend: When you're ready, doing a forward bend… Bending the knees slightly, and taking a deep breath in, stretching the arms up over the head, reaching up toward the ceiling, and then exhaling, pulling in at the abdominal muscles, and letting the body bend forward from the waist, the arms reaching toward the floor, knees are soft, slightly bent. Releasing the neck. And feeling the in-breath expanding the rib cage and then on the out-breath allowing the muscles to lengthen and relax. Letting the head sink down toward the knees and the floor, surrendering to the gravitational pull. And if you'd like to, inhaling and extending the right arm out, in front of you, parallel to the floor. The left arm and shoulder remain relaxed. Allowing the spine to lengthen. And then, exhaling and letting the arm come back down. Repeat on the other side. And when you're ready, beginning to come up slowly. Starting at the hips, the lower part of the spine, unwinding vertebra by vertebra. Becoming aware of how much of the spine you can experience as you do this. Return to mountain. Closing or lowering your eyes and sensing whatever is here, aware of the breath and everything else that is present in your internal and external landscape.

Chair Pose: And now we'll do the chair pose—inhaling and exhaling, stretching both arms out in front of you, feet a hip-width apart. Imagining that you're sitting down on a chair that is behind you, bending the knees, keeping the feet flat on the floor, heels down, keeping the head and back as straight as possible. And once you have come to rest in this position, breathing and balancing. Noticing the sensations present. And when you are ready, inhaling and slowly coming to a standing position, letting the arms drop and shaking the arms, shaking the legs, one at a time, taking a long deep breath, releasing all tension and discomfort on the out-breath, and allowing freshness and new life to come into the body with the in-breath.

[Bells]

Appendix B

Selected MBCT-Dual Tools

Weekly Rating Sheet

During each session, you will go over a fresh copy of this handout with your therapist. This helps you both keep track of how you are doing between sessions and identify what you may want to focus on in the sessions.

Your therapist will ask you to evaluate your **alcohol or drug use and other symptoms** using a 10-point scale where **1 = worst ever** and **10 = no longer a concern.**

Date: ______________________________

A. Ratings

SUBSTANCE USE: On the 10-point scale where **1 = worst ever** and **10 = no longer a concern**, how would you rate your alcohol or drug use **a week ago** and how would you rate it **now**?

__________ RATING A WEEK AGO __________ RATING NOW

How did you get from a ______ (number a week ago) to ______ (number today)?

____

If there has been a change, what do you think has increased or decreased your level of using drugs?

____

If there has been no change, what has kept it the same? ____________________

____

STRESS/PTSD (if applicable): How would you rate your stress or PTSD symptoms, where **1 = worst ever** and **10 = no longer a concern**?

__________ RATING A WEEK AGO __________ RATING NOW

How did you get from a ______ (number a week ago) to ______ (number today)?

____

If there has been a change, what do you think has increased or decreased your level of using drugs?

____

If there has been no change, what has kept it the same? ____________________

____

DEPRESSION (if applicable): How would you rate your depression, where **1 = worst ever** and **10 = no longer a concern**?

__________ **RATING A WEEK AGO** __________ **RATING NOW**

How did you get from a ______ (number a week ago) to ______ (number today)?

____

If there has been a change, what do you think has increased or decreased your level of using drugs?

____

If there has been no change, what has kept it the same? ____________________

ANXIETY (if applicable): How would you rate your anxiety symptoms, where **1 = worst ever** and **10 = no longer a concern**?

__________ **RATING A WEEK AGO** __________ **RATING NOW**

How did you get from a ______ (number a week ago) to ______ (number today)?

____

If there has been a change, what do you think has increased or decreased your level of using drugs?

____

If there has been no change, what has kept it the same? ____________________

____

Have you been noticing any thoughts, feelings, or body sensations during this week that led to your ratings above?

____

Is there anything that you want to make sure we focus on today and in our next sessions?

____

B. Preparation for next meeting

To prepare for your next meeeting with your therapist, review and consider the following:

This past week I used or had thoughts about using…
(Check all that apply.)

______ When I felt the need to cope

______ When I just wanted to have fun

______ Out of habit

______ Other ______________________________

My goals for next session are…
(Check all that apply.)

______ Not to use substances

______ Reduce my use of substances

______ Work on one of my life goals

______ Work on my stressful situations or feelings

______ Other ____

Things to consider between and before sessions:

What situations or feelings bothered me in the past week?

What do I most want to share with my therapist?

What types of changes have I noticed in myself?

What worked for me in the past week?

What are the changes I want?

How confident do I feel about making those changes?

How can I feel more confident about making those changes?

STOP Technique:

Stop or pause

Take a breath

Observe, open, soften

Proceed when you feel centered

Stop Light Metaphor

Don't act.

Notice how your body feels. Notice your emotions.

When you feel balanced, in control and able to respond: Proceed

Appendix C

Guidelines for Behavior Rehearsal Role-Play

The main factor that determines the success of cognitive skills training is the extent to which clients practice and apply the new skills in their lives. For instance, during the weekly ratings discussion, a client may describe a recent relapse precipitated by an offer of marijuana. The therapist can encourage role-playing in which the client responds by refusing the offer. Or, during a later discussion of requesting help and support, the therapist can ask a client to role-play asking for help. Role-play can also be helpful when developing coping strategies and plans for dealing with triggers and generating PTSD-related cognitive restructuring action plans.

Practicing how to respond to real-life situations is a powerful adjunct to treatment because it enhances the likelihood that these behaviors will be repeated in similar situations (i.e., generalization) and in the context of the adolescent's life. Practice exercises can be modified to fit the specific details of individual situations.

Some clients and/or therapists may feel uncomfortable or embarrassed at first about role-playing. As a result, it may be tempting for the therapist to allow the adolescent to talk about the skills rather than practice them, which would decrease the effectiveness of therapy. Therapists can increase the likelihood that clients will participate in role-plays by taking the lead in the first one. Therapists should acknowledge that feelings of awkwardness are normal when trying a new interpersonal behavior such as role-play. Here are suggested basic steps for conducting role-plays:

1. **Explain what role-playing is,** if you have not already done so. Keep in mind that many clients are likely to be familiar with the idea of role-play, so it may not require a long explanation. For example, you might say,

   I'd like you to practice turning down an offer to smoke by doing that here with me, as if you were acting. The first time, I'll pretend to be that guy you told me about.

2. **Briefly review the situation to be role-played.** What is the problem? What is the skill to be practiced?

   Okay, so your friend is driving you to school, and she offers to get high with you. You turn down the offer.

3. **Determine who will play which role.** Suggestions for acting the part can be solicited and offered.

   I can play your mom, Jason. Should I act mad, sad, or what?

Role reversal is a role-play strategy in which the therapist models use of the new skill, with the client playing the role of the friend, parent, or teacher. This strategy is particularly useful if a client is having difficulty using a skill or is pessimistic about the effectiveness of a suggested approach. By playing the "other," he or she has an opportunity to observe and experience firsthand the effects of the suggested skill.

4. **Create role-play scenarios.** The following strategies are useful in helping clients generate scenes:

   - Ask clients to recall a situation in the recent past where use of the skills being taught would have been desirable.
   - Ask clients to anticipate a difficult situation that may arise in the near future that calls for use of the skill.
   - Request that clients write down scenarios to be role-played.
   - Suggest appropriate situations based on knowledge of clients' recent circumstances.

5. **Enact the role-play.** Encourage clients to be assertive and clear about what they are saying and asking during an interaction.

6. **Process the role-play.** After a role-play has been enacted, it is essential that it be effectively processed. This is an opportunity for clients to receive praise and recognition for practice and improvement, as well as constructive feedback about the less effective elements of their attempt. Initial attempts may show few elements of the communication skill being taught. During this portion of the session, the therapist's primary goal is to look for successful elements of the skill and to reinforce those elements. The primary emphasis should be on what the

client is doing well, in order to gradually shape his or her behavior in a positive direction. A secondary focus is making limited suggestions for improvement. Following are the procedures for delivering this feedback:

- Immediately after every role-play, both therapist and client should give their reactions to the performance. Examples: How do the protagonists feel about the way they handled the situation? What effect did the interaction have on the other?
- The praise and reinforcement provided should always be sincere. However, the therapist should refrain from being unnecessarily effusive so that the value of the positive feedback is not undermined.
- The scene should be repeated to give the client an opportunity to try out the feedback he or she received the first time around.

Appendix D

Poetry in Mindfulness

One of the best tools in mindfulness practice today is poetry. Why? Because the very act of reading a poem cultivates mindfulness. To fully experience any poem, we must stop whatever we are doing and give it our full attention, from start to finish, just as the poet did when writing it. The following are some poems to get you started with using poetry in your mindfulness practice. Poetry and music are excellent ways to express thoughts and feelings and to delve into our experiences. Start with these poems, and then begin to collect some of your own poems and music lyrics to use in mindfulness practice.

"Kindness," by Naomi Shihab Nye. Available in Nye, N. S. (1994). *Words Under the Words: Selected Poems by Naomi Shihab Nye*. Portland, OR: The Eighth Mountain Press.

"Love After Love," by Derek Walcott. Available in Walcott, D. (1976). *Sea Grapes*. New York, NY: Farrar, Straus, and Giroux.

"The Guest House" and "Two Kinds of Intelligence," by Rumi. Available in Rumi (1997). *The Essential Rumi* (C. Barks, Trans.). New York, NY: Harper Collins.

"The Holy Longing," (excerpt) by Goethe. Available in Bly, R. (Ed. and Trans., 1980). *News of the Universe: Poems of Twofold Consciousness*. San Francisco, CA: Sierra Club Books.

"The Invitation," by Oriah Mountain Dreamer. Available in Oriah Mountain Dreamer (1997). *The Invitation*. San Francisco, CA: HarperOne. http://www.oriah.org

"Wild Geese," by Mary Oliver. Available in Oliver, M. (1986). *Dream Work*. New York, NY: Atlantic Monthly Press.

References

Amaro, H., & Vallejo, Z. (2008). Moment-by-moment in women's recovery: A mindfulness-based approach to relapse prevention (MBRP-W). Boston, MA: Institute on Urban Health Research, Northeastern University and Boston Public Health Commission.

American Psychiatric Association. (2013). *Diagnostic and statistical manual of mental disorders (5th ed.)*. Arlington, VA: Author. http://dx.doi.org/10.1176/appi.books.9780890425596

Ameringer, K. J., & Leventhal, A. M. (2012). Symptom dimensions of attention deficit hyperactivity disorder and nicotine withdrawal symptoms. *Journal of Addictive Diseases, 31*(4), 363–75. http://dx.doi.org/10.1080/10550887.2012.735568

Baer, R. A. (2003). Mindfulness training as a clinical intervention: A conceptual and empirical review. *Clinical Psychology: Science & Practice, 10*(2), 125–143. http://dx.doi.org/10.1093/clipsy.bpg015

Barnhofer, T., & Chittka, T. (2009). Cognitive reactivity mediates the relationship between neuroticism and depression. *Behavior Research and Therapy, 48*(4), 275–281. http://dx.doi.org/10.1016/j.brat.2009.12.005

Bechara, A., & Naqvi, N. (2004). Listening to your Heart: Interoceptive awareness as a gateway to feeling. *Nature Neuroscience, 7,* 102–103. http://dx.doi.org/10.1038/nn0204-102

Beck, A. T., Rush, A. J., Shaw, B. F., & Emery, G. (1979). *Cognitive therapy of depression.* New York, NY: Guilford.

Benoit, M. (1993). Impact of violence on children and adolescents: Report from a community-based child psychiatry clinic. *Psychiatry, 56*(1), 124–126.

Black, D. S., Sussman, S., Johnson, C. A., & Milam, J. (2012). Psychometric assessment of the Mindful Attention Awareness Scale (MAAS) among Chinese adolescents. *Assessment, 19*(1), 42–52. http://dx.doi.org/10.1177/1073191111415365

Bonn-Miller, M. O., Vujanovic, A. A., Feldner, M. T., Bernstein, A., & Zvolensky, M. J. (2007). Posttraumatic stress symptom severity predicts marijuana use coping motives among traumatic event-exposed marijuana users. *Journal of Traumatic Stress, 20*(4), 577–586. http://dx.doi.org/10.1002/jts.20243

Bowen, S., Chawla, N., & Marlatt, G. A. (2011). *Mindfulness-based relapse prevention for addictive behaviors: A clinician's guide.* New York, NY: The Guilford Press.

Brown, K. W., & Ryan, R. M. (2003). The benefits of being present: Mindfulness and its role in psychological well-being. *Journal of Personality and Social Psychology, 84*(4), 822–848. http://dx.doi.org/10.1037/0022-3514.84.4.822

Brown, K. W., Ryan, R. M., & Creswell, J. D. (2007). Mindfulness: Theoretical foundations and evidence for its salutary effects. *Psychological Inquiry, 18*(4), 211–237. http://dx.doi.org/10.1080/10478400701598298

Burns, D. D. (1989). *The feeling good handbook.* New York, NY: Penguin Books.

Caffo, E., & Belaise, C. (2003). Psychological aspects of traumatic injury in children and adolescents. *Child and Adolescent Psychiatric Clinics of North America, 12*(3): 493–535.

Carroll, S., Hides, L., Catania, L., Mathias, S., Greenwood-Smith, C., & Lubman, D. (2009). Integrated cognitive behaviour therapy for co-occurring substance misuse and major depression: Lessons from a youth mental health service. *Australasian Psychiatry, 17*(5), 365–370. http://dx.doi.org/10.1080/10398560902912544

Carver, C. S., & Scheier, M. F. (2011). Self-regulation of action and affect. In K. D. Vohs and R. F. Baumeister (Eds.), *Handbook of self-regulation: Research, theory, and applications* (2nd ed., pp. 3–21). New York, NY: Guilford.

Cohen, J. A., Mannarino, A. P., & Staron, V. R. (2006). A pilot study of modified cognitive-behavioral therapy for childhood traumatic grief (CBT-CTG). *Journal of the American Academy of Child and Adolescent Psychiatry, 45*(12), 1465–1473. http://dx.doi.org/10.1097/01.chi.0000237705.43260.2c

Cohen, J. A., Mannarino, A. P., Zhitova, A. C., & Capone, M. E. (2003). Treating child abuse-related posttraumatic stress and comorbid substance abuse in adolescents. *Child Abuse and Neglect, 27*(12), 1345–1365. http://dx.doi.org/10.1016/j.chiabu.2003.08.001

Decety, J., & Jackson, P. L. (2004). The functional architecture of human empathy. *Behavioral and Cognitive Neuroscience Reviews, 3*(2), 71–100.

Dorsey, S., Briggs, E. C., & Woods, B. A. (2011). Cognitive-behavioral treatment for posttraumatic stress disorder in children and adolescents. *Child and Adolescent Psychiatric Clinics of North America, 20*(2), 255–269. http://dx.doi.org/10.1016/j.chc.2011.01.006

Foa, E. B., Ehlers, A., Clark, D. M., Tolin, D. F., & Orsillo, S. M. (1999). The Posttraumatic Cognitions Inventory (PTCI): Development and validation. *Psychological Assessment, 11*(3), 303–314. http://dx.doi.org/10.1037//1040-3590.11.3.303

Fortuna, L. R., Porche, M. V., & Ziedonis, D. (2013). A pilot study of cognitive behavioral therapy for co-occurring PTSD and substance use disorders with multicultural youth in the community. Manuscript in preparation.

Garland, E. L., Gaylord, S. A., & Fredrickson, B. L. (2011). Positive reappraisal mediates the stress-reductive effects of mindfulness: An upward spiral process. *Mindfulness, 2*(1), 59–67. http://dx.doi.org/10.1007/s12671-011-0043-8

Garrison, K. A., Scheinost, D., Constable, R. T., & Brewer, J. A. (2014). BOLD signal and functional connectivity associated with loving kindness meditation. *Brain and Behavior, 4*(3), 337–347. http://dx.doi.org/10.1002/brb3.219

Germer, C. (2009). *The mindful path to self-compassion: Freeing yourself from destructive thoughts and emotions*. New York, NY: Guilford.

Godfrin, K. A., & van Heeringen, C. (2010). The effects of mindfulness-based cognitive therapy on recurrence of depressive episodes, mental health and quality of life: A randomized controlled study. *Behaviour Research and Therapy, 48*(8), 738–746. http://dx.doi.org/10.1016/j.brat.2010.04.006

Goldstein, J., & Kornfield, J. (1987). *Seeking the heart of wisdom: The path of insight meditation*. Boston, MA: Shambhala.

Grossman, P., Niemann, L., Schmidt, S., & Walach, H. (2004). Mindfulness-based stress reduction and health benefits. A meta-analysis. *Journal of Psychosomatic Research, 57*(1), 35–43. http://dx.doi.org/10.1016/s0022-3999(03)00573-7

Hamblen, J. L., Norris, F. H., Pietruszkiewicz, S., Gibson, L. E., Naturale, A., & Louis, C. (2009). Cognitive behavioral therapy for postdisaster distress: A community based treatment program for survivors of Hurricane Katrina. *Administration and Policy in Mental Health and Mental Health Services Research, 36*(3), 206–214. http://dx.doi.org/10.1007/s10488-009-0213-3

Hides, L., Samet, S., & Lubman, D. I. (2010). Cognitive behaviour therapy (CBT) for the treatment of co-occurring depression and substance use: Current evidence and directions for future research. *Drug and Alcohol Review, 29*(5), 508–517. http://dx.doi.org/10.1111/j.1465-3362.2010.00207.x

Hofmann, S. G., Sawyer, A. T., Witt, A. A., & Oh, D. (2010). The effect of mindfulness-based therapy on anxiety and depression: A meta-analytic review. *Journal of Consulting and Clinical Psychology, 78*(2), 169–183. http://dx.doi.org/10.1037/a0018555

Huestis, M. A., Mitchell, J. M., & Cone, E. J. (1996). Urinary excretion profiles of 11-nor-9-carboxy-delta 9-tetrahydrocannabinol in humans after single smoked doses of marijuana. *Journal of Analytic Toxicology, 20*(6), 441–452. http://dx.doi.org/10.1093/jat/20.6.441

James, A., Soler, A., & Weatherall, R. (2005). Cognitive behavioural therapy for anxiety disorders in children and adolescents. *Cochrane Database of Systematic Reviews*, (4), CD004690. http://dx.doi.org/10.1002/14651858.cd004690.pub2

Jha, A. P., Krompinger, J., & Baime, M. J. (2007). Mindfulness training modifies subsystems of attention. *Cognitive, Affective, and Behavioral Neuroscience, 7*(2), 109–119. http://dx.doi.org/10.3758/cabn.7.2.109

Kabat-Zinn, J. (1996). Mindfulness meditation: What it is, what it isn't, and its role in health care and medicine. In Y. Haruli, Y. Ishii, & M. Suzuki (Eds.), *Comparative and Psychological Study on Meditation* (pp. 161–169). The Netherlands: Eburon.

Kabat-Zinn, J. (2005). Bringing mindfulness to medicine: An interview with Jon Kabat-Zinn, PhD. Interview by Karolyn Gazella. *Advances in Mind-Body Medicine, 21*(2), 22–27.

Kabat-Zinn, J. (2013). *Full Catastrophe Living: Using the Wisdom of Your Body and Mind to Face Stress, Pain, and Illness*. New York, NY: Bantam Books. (Original work published 1990)

Kaminer, Y., Bukstein, O., & Tarter, R. E. (1991). The Teen-Addiction Severity Index: Rationale and reliability. *International Journal of the Addictions, 26*(2), 219–226.

Kaminer, Y., Burleson, J. A., & Goldberger, R. (2002). Cognitive-behavioral coping skills and psychoeducation therapies for adolescent substance abuse. *The Journal of Nervous and Mental Disease, 190*(11), 737–745. http://dx.doi.org/10.1097/00005053-200211000-00003

Karver, M. S., Handelsman, J. B., Fields, S., & Bickman, L. (2006). Meta-analysis of therapeutic relationship variables in youth and family therapy: The evidence for different relationship variables in the child and adolescent treatment outcome literature. *Clinical Psychology Review, 26*(1), 50–65. http://dx.doi.org/10.1016/j.cpr.2005.09.001

Kessler, R. C., Berglund, P., Demler, O., Jin, R., Merikangas, K. R., & Walters, E. E. (2005). Lifetime prevalence and age-of-onset distributions of DSM-IV disorders in the National Comorbidity Survey Replication. *Archives of General Psychiatry, 62*(6), 593–602. http://dx.doi.org/10.1001/archpsyc.62.6.593

Killingsworth, M. A., & Gilbert, D. T. (2010). A wandering mind is an unhappy mind. *Science, 330*(2010): 932.

Kilpatrick, D. G., Acierno, R., Saunders, B., Resnick, H. S., Best, C. L., & Schnurr, P. P. (2000). Risk factors for adolescent substance abuse and dependence: Data from a national sample. *Journal of Consulting and Clinical Psychology*, 68(1), 19–30. http://dx.doi.org/10.1037//0022-006x.68.1.19

Kobasa, S. C. (1979). Stressful life events, personality, and health: An inquiry into hardiness. *Journal of Personality and Social Psychology, 37*(1), 1–11. http://dx.doi.org/10.1037//0022-3514.37.1.1

Kramer, G. (2007). *Insight dialogue: The interpersonal path to freedom*. Boston, MA: Shambhala.

Kravariti, E., Schulze, K., Kane, F., Kalidindi, S., Bramon, E., Walshe, M., …Murray, R. M. (2009). Stroop-test interference in bipolar disorder. *British Journal of Psychiatry, 194*(3), 285–286. http://dx.doi.org/10.1192/bjp.bp.108.052639

Kuyken, W., Watkins, E., Holden, E., White, K., Taylor, R. S., Byford, S., …Dalgleish, T. (2010). How does mindfulness-based cognitive therapy work? *Behaviour Research and Therapy, 48(11)*, 1105–1112. http://dx.doi.org/10.1016/j.brat.2010.08.003

Lee, C. T., Fuemmeler, B. F., McClernon, F. J., Ashley-Koch, A., & Kollins, S. H. (2013). Nicotinic receptor gene variants interact with attention deficient hyperactive disorder symptoms to predict smoking trajectories from early adolescence to adulthood. *Addictive Behaviors*, 38(11), 2683–2689. http://dx.doi.org/10.1016/j.addbeh.2013.06.013

Levine, P., & Mate, G. (2010). *In an unspoken voice: How the body releases trauma and restores goodness*. Berkley, CA: North Atlantic Books.

Lipschitz, D. S., Rasmusson, A. M., Anyan, W., Gueorguieva, R., Billingslea, E. M., Cromwell, P. F., & Southwick, S. M. (2003). Posttraumatic stress disorder and substance use in inner-city adolescent girls. *The Journal of Nervous and Mental Disease, 191*(11), 714–721. http://dx.doi.org/10.1097/01.nmd.0000095123.68088.da

Luthar, S. S., Cicchetti, D., & Becker, B. (2000). The construct of resilience: A critical evaluation and guidelines for future work. *Child Development, 71*(3), 543–562. http://dx.doi.org/10.1111/1467-8624.00164

Lutz, A., Slagter, H. A., Dunne, J. D., & Davidson, R. J. (2008). Attention regulation and monitoring in meditation. *Trends in Cognitive Science, 12*(4), 163–169. http://dx.doi.org/10.1016/j.tics.2008.01.005

Maalouf, F. T., Klein, C., Clark, L., Sahakian, B. J., LaBarbara, E. J., Versace, A., … Phillips, M. L. (2010). Impaired sustained attention and executive dysfunction: Bipolar disorder versus depression-specific markers of affective disorders. *Neuropsychologica, 48*(6), 1862–1868. http://dx.doi.org/10.1016/j.neuropsychologia.2010.02.015

Marks I., Lovell, K., Noshirvani, H., Livanou, M., & Thrasher, S. (1998). Treatment of posttraumatic stress disorder by exposure and/or cognitive restructuring: A controlled study. *Archives of General Psychiatry*, 55(4), 317–325. http://dx.doi.org/10.1001/archpsyc.55.4.317

McGovern, M. P., Lambert-Harris, C., Acquilano, S., Xie, H., Alterman, A. I., & Weiss, R. D. (2009). A cognitive behavioral therapy for co-occurring substance use and posttraumatic stress disorders. *Addictive Behaviors, 34*(10), 892–897. http://dx.doi.org/10.1016/j.addbeh.2009.03.009

Miller, C. E., & Johnson, J. L. (2001). Motivational interviewing. *The Canadian Nurse*, 97(7), 32–33.

Miller, W. R. (1996). Motivational interviewing: Research, practice, and puzzles. *Addictive Behaviors, 21*(6), 835–842. http://dx.doi.org/10.1016/0306-4603(96)00044-5

Miller, W. R., & Rollnick, S. (2012). *Motivational interviewing: Helping people change* (3rd ed.) New York, NY: Guilford Press.

Miller, W. R., & Rose, G. S. (2009). Toward a theory of motivational interviewing. *American Psychologist*, 64(6), 527–537. http://dx.doi.org/10.1037/a0016830

Miller, W. R., Yahne, C. E., & Tonigan, J. S. (2003). Motivational interviewing in drug abuse services: A randomized trial. *Journal of Consulting and Clinical Psychology, 71*(4), 754–763. http://dx.doi.org/10.1037/0022-006x.71.4.754

Moyers, T. B., Martin, T., Manuel, J. K., Hendrickson, S. M., & Miller, W. R. (2005). Assessing competence in the use of motivational interviewing. *Journal of Substance Abuse Treatment*, 28(1), 19–26. http://dx.doi.org/10.1016/j.jsat.2004.11.001

Mueser, K.T., Rosenberg, S. D., & Rosenberg, H. J. (2009). *Treatment of posttraumatic stress disorder in special populations: A cognitive restructuring program*. Washington, DC: American Psychological Association. http://dx.doi.org/10.1037/11889-000

Mueser, K. T., Rosenberg, S. D., Xie, H., Jankowski, M. K., Bolton, E. E., Lu, W., …Wolfe, R. (2008). A randomized controlled trial of cognitive-behavioral treatment for posttraumatic stress disorder in severe mental illness. *Journal of Consulting and Clinical Psychology*, *76*(2), 259–271. http://dx.doi.org/10.1037/0022-006x.76.2.259

Neff, K. D. (2003) The development and validation of a scale to measure self-compassion. *Self and Identity*, *2*(3), 223–250. http://dx.doi.org/10.1080/15298860309027

Neff, K. D. (2011). *Self-compassion: The proven power of being kind to yourself.* New York, NY: Harper Collins.

Neff, K. D., & Mcgehee, P. (2010). Self-compassion and psychological resilience among adolescents and young adults. *Self and Identity*, *9*(3): 225–240.

Pagnoni, G., & Cekic, M. (2007). Age effects on gray matter volume and attentional performance in Zen meditation. *Neurobiology of Aging*. *28*(10), 1623–1627. http://dx.doi.org/10.1016/j.neurobiolaging.2007.06.008

Porges, S. W. (2009). The polyvagal theory: New insights into adaptive reactions of the autonomic nervous system. *Cleveland Clinic Journal of Medicine*, *76*(Suppl 2), S86–S90. http://dx.doi.org/10.3949/ccjm.76.s2.17

Porges, S. W., & Furman, S. A. (2011). The early development of the autonomic nervous system provides a neural platform for social behavior: A polyvagal perspective. *Infant and Child Development*, *20*(1), 106–118. http://dx.doi.org/10.1002/icd.688

Roemer, L., Orsillo, S. M., & Salters-Pedneault, K. (2008). Efficacy of an acceptance-based behavior therapy for generalized anxiety disorder: Evaluation in a randomized controlled trial. *Journal of Consulting and Clinical Psychology*, *76*(6), 1083–1089. http://dx.doi.org/10.1037/a0012720

Rollnick, S., Butler, C. C., Kinnersley, P., Gregory, J., & Mash, B. (2010). Motivational interviewing. *British Medical Journal*, 2010;340:c1900. http://dx.doi.org/10.1136/bmj.c1900

Rosenberg, H. J., Jankowski, M. K., Fortuna, L. R., Rosenberg, S. D., & Mueser, K. T. (2011). A pilot study of a cognitive restructuring program for treating posttraumatic disorders in adolescents. *Psychological Trauma: Theory, Research, Practice, and Policy*, *3*(1), 94–99. http://dx.doi.org/10.1037/a0019889

Salmon, P., Lush, E., Jablonski, M. & Sephton, S. E. (2009). Yoga and mindfulness: Clinical aspects of an ancient mind/body practice. *Cognitive and Behavioral Practice*, *16*(1): 59–72.

Salzberg, S. (2013). Mindfulness and loving-kindness. In M. G. Williams & J. Kabat-Zinn (Eds.), *Mindfulness: Diverse perspectives on its meaning, origins, and applications*. New York, NY: Routledge.

Sampl, S., & Kadden, R. (2001). Motivational enhancement therapy and cognitive behavioral therapy for adolescent cannabis users: 5 sessions. Cannabis Youth Treatment (CYT) Series, Volume 1 (DHHS Publication No. (SMA) 01-3846). Rockville, MD: Center for Substance Abuse Treatment, Substance Abuse and Mental Health Services Administration.

Santorelli, S. (1999). *Heal thy self: Lessons on mindfulness in medicine*. New York, NY: Bell Tower.

Schouela, D. (2014). *Clinical insights from the polyvagal theory* (unpublished manuscript). Trauma Center. Brookline, MA.

Schuman-Olivier, Z., Albanese, M., Carlini, S., & Shaffer, H. J. (2010, December). *Effects of trait mindfulness during Buprenorphine treatment for heroin dependence: A pilot study.* Poster presented at the AAAP 21st annual meeting, Boca Raton, FL.

Segal Z. V., Bieling, P., Young, T., MacQueen, G., Cooke, R., Martin, L., Bloch, R., Levitan, R. D. (2010). Antidepressant monotherapy vs. sequential pharmacotherapy and mindfulness-based cognitive therapy, or placebo, for relapse prophylaxis in recurrent depression. *Archives of General Psychiatry, 67*(12), 1256–1264.

Segal, Z. V., Williams, J. M. G, & Teasdale, J. D. (2002). *Mindfulness-based cognitive therapy for depression: A new approach to preventing relapse*. New York, NY: The Guilford Press.

Segal, Z., Williams, J. M. G., & Teasdale, J. D. (2013). *Mindfulness-based cognitive therapy for depression, Second Edition*. New York, NY: The Guilford Press.

Shapiro, D. H., Jr. (1982). Overview: Clinical and physiological comparison of meditation with other self-control strategies. *American Journal of Psychiatry, 139*(3), 267–274. http://dx.doi.org/10.1176/ajp.139.3.267

Shapiro, S. L., Carlson, L. E., Astin, J. A., & Freedman, B. (2006). Mechanisms of mindfulness. *Journal of Clinical Psychology, 62*(3), 373–386. http://dx.doi.org/10.1002/jclp.20237

Siegel, D. J. (2007). *The mindful brain: Reflection and attunement in the cultivation of well-being*. New York, NY: W.W. Norton & Company.

Siegel, D. J. (2010). *Mindsight: The new science of personal transformation*. New York, NY: Bantam Books.

Singer, T., Seymour, B., O'Doherty, J., Kaube, H., Dolan, R., & Frith, C. (2004). Empathy for pain involves the affective but not sensory components of pain. *Science, 303*(5661), 1157–1162. http://dx.doi.org/10.1126/science.1093535

Stahl, B., & Goldstein, E. (2010). *A mindfulness-based stress reduction workbook*. Oakland, CA: New Harbinger Publications.

Stevens, S. J., Murphy, B. S., & McKnight, K. (2003). Traumatic stress and gender differences in relationship to substance abuse, mental health, physical health, and HIV risk behavior in a sample of adolescents enrolled in drug treatment. *Child Maltreatment*, 8(1), 46–57. http://dx.doi.org/10.1177/1077559502239611

Tan, C. M. (2012). *Search inside yourself: The unexpected path to achieving success, happiness (and world peace)*. New York, NY: HarperOne.

Teasdale, J. D., Segal, Z. V., Williams, J. M. G., Ridgeway, V. A., Soulsby, J. M., & Lau, M. A. (2000). Prevention of relapse/recurrence in major depression by mindfulness-based cognitive therapy. *Journal of Consulting and Clinical Psychology, 68*(4), 615–623. http://dx.doi.org/10.1037//0022-006x.68.4.615

Valentine, E. R., & Sweet, P. L. G. (1999). Meditation and attention: A comparison of the effects of concentrative and mindfulness meditation on sustained attention. *Mental Health, Religion and Culture, 2*(1), 59–70. http://dx.doi.org/10.1080/13674679908406332

Vallejo Z., & Amaro, H. (2009). Adaptation of mindfulness-based stress reduction program for addiction relapse prevention. *The Humanistic Psychologist, 37*(2), 192–206. http://dx.doi.org/10.1080/08873260902892287

Van Dam, N. T., Sheppard, S. C., Forsyth, J. P., & Earleywine, M. (2011). Self-compassion is a better predictor than mindfulness of symptom severity and quality of life in mixed anxiety and depression. *Journal of Anxiety Disorders, 25*(1), 123–130. http://dx.doi.org/10.1016/j.janxdis.2010.08.011

Waldron, H. B., Kern-Jones, S., Turner, C. W., Peterson, T. R., & Ozechowski, T. J. (2007). Engaging resistant adolescents in drug abuse treatment. *Journal of Substance Abuse Treatment, 32*(2), 133–142. http://dx.doi.org/10.1016/j.jsat.2006.07.007

Williams, M., & Penman, D. (2011). *Mindfulness: An eight-week plan for finding peace in a frantic world*. New York, NY: Rodale.

Lisa R. Fortuna, MD, is a board-certified child and adolescent psychiatrist with over fifteen years of clinical experience with children, adolescents, and families. She is currently faculty at Boston University School of Medicine and medical director of Child and Adolescent Psychiatry at Boston Medical Center. She has published highly cited articles in the areas of post-traumatic stress disorder (PTSD), adolescent substance abuse, and Latino and immigrant mental health. Fortuna received a K23 Patient Oriented Career Development Award from the National Institute on Drug Abuse (NIDA) to develop a cognitive behavioral therapy intervention for adolescents with co-occurring trauma and addictions, which formed the basis for this book. She continues to conduct research in post-traumatic stress, depression, and substance abuse, and to develop health services programs for adolescents facing these problems.

Zayda Vallejo, MLitt, is a certified senior teacher in mindfulness-based stress reduction (MBSR) adjunct faculty at the Center for Mindfulness in Medicine, Health Care, and Society at the University of Massachusetts Medical School. For a decade and a half, she has provided MBSR training to professionals aspiring to teach and mentor in diverse health settings and to various populations. She has codeveloped customized curricula for mindfulness-based interventions for women in recovery to cope with the myriad of stresses in their lives, for Tourette's syndrome, for intimate partner violence (in process), and for primary care (in process). Vallejo has also consulted on neuroscientific studies conducted by Harvard University's Lazar Lab for Meditation Research.

Foreword writer **Florence Meleo-Meyer, MS, MA,** is director of the Oasis Institute for Mindfulness-Based Professional Education and Training at the Center for Mindfulness in Medicine, Health Care, and Society at the University of Massachusetts Medical School. She is a leading international teacher who has helped develop and offer professional trainings for MBSR teachers for over eighteen years. In addition to teaching in the MBSR program, she has offered mindfulness programs to educators, physicians, psychologists, and young adults.

Index

H

I

J

K

L

M

N

O

P

Q

R

S

T

U

V

W